EGG ON YOUR INTERFACE

EGG
ON YOUR
INTERFACE

A Dictionary of Modern Nonsense

PATRICK SCRIVENOR

BUCHAN & ENRIGHT, PUBLISHERS

First published in 1989 by
Buchan & Enright, Publishers (Fountain Press Ltd)
45 The Broadway, Tolworth, Surrey KT6 7DW

British Library Cataloguing in Publication Data

Scrivenor, Patrick, *1943*–
Egg on your interface ; a dictionary of
modern nonsense.
1. English language. Usage
I. Title
428

ISBN 0-907675-89-1

Photoset in North Wales by
Derek Doyle & Associates, Mold, Clwyd
Printed and Bound in Great Britain by
Hartnolls Limited, Bodmin, Cornwall.

To all those friends who will find between these covers jokes at which they have laughed – with heroic forbearance – at least five or six times already.

ACKNOWLEDGEMENTS

I am greatly indebted to my colleague Hugh Bredin for the title of this book – by far the funniest thing in it – and for the entries MEGO and WYSIWYG, which I am more and more inclined to believe he invented. I am also indebted to my uncle, The Rev. Peter Murray, who many years ago gave me the first definition of EDUCATION reproduced here. I must thank my colleague Mark Le Fanu who did his best to put me wise to the baffling intricacies of POST STRUCTURALISM. The derivation I suggest for the word F*** is not my own, but since the colleague who provided it is both female and married she might be embarrassed by an attribution, and I have gallantly assumed all the discredit myself. The entries INSTANTANEOUS DISASSEMBLY and RAPID OXIDATION were provided by Tony Hernandez, a keen aficionado of verbal absurdity. The entries under ECONOMIST and ECONOMY were given to me by Patrick Burgess.

As far as I know all other witticisms and attempted witticisms in this book are original, but under the combined influences of DISCOURSE and INTERTEXTUALITY I may have blundered into unconscious plagiarism.

Above all I am indebted to my friend Don Yoder, who read the typescript, and bears in general the heavy responsibility of having encouraged me to write.

Lastly I would like to thank my dog, who has patiently forgone many walks in the interests of an activity which, he has made very plain, he regards as entirely otiose.

INTRODUCTION

The misuse of language is so widespread that there seems little hope of turning back the tide. Certainly in those quarters from which one expects help – the universities, the Church, the professions – none is to be found. They scatter the horrible new polysyllables about with prodigal abandon, and for an obvious reason. They have a vested interest in earnestness.

Language is too enjoyable a matter to leave to professionals – especially professional linguists. They take it seriously, and the results are calamitous. It is time for the enthusiastic amateur to take a hand, and I am confident that no-one will challenge the amateur status of this dictionary.

Many readers will find it an eccentric dictionary. It is certainly not scholarly. It is not intended to be a guide to good English, but I hope I have supplied enough bad English to give the reader a hearty laugh.

As for being a Dictionary of Modern Nonsense, it is. But the reader will not fail to notice that much of the nonsense is my own, and that a few of the entries are not modern nonsense in the purest sense at all. I cannot help it. It would take a man of stone to confront the output of the modern mind without occasionally resorting to frivolity.

I had some qualms about including entries under the five main religions, on the grounds that by categorising them as nonsense I might be giving offence. However, I took courage from the unfailingly bitter and sectarian nature of religious enthusiasm, and I urge the believer to look up every entry except his own. By this simple expedient he will find himself in full agreement with me.

I have also included definitions that are not my own (see

Acknowledgements) on the grounds that (a) they are funny, (b) I haven't seen them in print, and (c) on both counts they deserve the permanence of black ink before they are lost.

There is a temptation to shrug off the abuse of English as a matter of little importance. 'Meaning will out' marches beside 'Usage is all' to lull us into accepting the frightful barbarisms spawned by the moderns.

But meaning will not necessarily out, as anyone who has tried to put pen to paper for a living knows. To write clear English requires clear thought and at least a reasonable command of vocabulary and grammar.

As for the usage argument, usage by whom? Does the fad among businessmen and estate agents for using the word PRESTIGIOUS to mean 'having prestige' really establish that as its meaning? Obviously not. The claims of precedence and lexicography are at least equal, if not superior.

The rules of writing good English are not very complicated. There is little to add to George Orwell's essay *Politics and the English Language*; to Sir Ernest Gower's *Plain Words*; or to Fowler's *English Usage*. Certainly I can add nothing, but there is one weapon that I can bring to bear against the enemies of good English, and that is ridicule.

It is right to ridicule certain habits of mind – above all earnestness. In retrospect it seems unjust of Dr Johnson to have ridiculed Bruce, the Abyssinian explorer. Bruce had indeed been to Abyssinia, as he claimed, and his account of it was accurate. Furthermore, Johnson must at least be suspected of pique on behalf of his novel *Rasselas*, which presented an entirely different picture of Abyssinia. Nonetheless Bruce's haughty and evasive manner would have excited suspicion in one far less alert to humbug than Johnson, and if Johnson had been less ready to mock pretence, wrongly in the case of Bruce, he would have been less quick to spot the Ossian imposture.

Ridicule is a shotgun. In the heat of the battle we must expect a few beaters to get hit.

I am therefore unrepentant of my facetious approach to what some would call a serious subject. Seriousness is a disease, and one of the most noticeable characteristics of diseased language is that it is serious.

What is special about *modern* nonsense? Pretentious speech and writing are as old as civilisation. The circumlocution of officials, the humbug of demagogues, and the jargon of cliques have been held up to ridicule throughout history. There have always been people who see language not as a pane through which light can pass uncorrupted, but as a useful distorting glass, to bend, reflect, or otherwise misdirect the light.

Since the last war, nonsense has acquired an unmistakable tone, in which diffusion of meaning and flatness of rhythm combine to make language a narcotic rather than a stimulant. Modern nonsense is also distinct from ancient nonsense in being a worldwide epidemic. It has affected every part of the civilised world, and Cambridge. It is, partly at any rate, the result of a phenomenon unique to the twentieth century – widespread partial education.

Real, resounding nonsense is not the province of the uneducated man. Lack of formal education is no bar to clear self expression. When Sam Goldwyn said 'Include me out', or when General Andrew Jackson at the Battle of New Orleans said 'Elevate them guns a little lower', it would have been an obtuse listener who did not understand them. Besides, the uneducated, since they pick up most of their language by ear, uually have a pronounced sense of rhythm. And it is by rhythm, by adapting the sound of words to the tenor of your thoughts, that meaning begins to be expressed. The loss of rhythm is a marked characteristic of modern nonsense.

No. Modern nonsense is caused by *incomplete* education. It is rife in America, where every citizen is educated to a level somewhere beween school and university (a notoriously feeble phase of human development), and where to lack seriousness is a far graver social offence than to lack continence.

Modern nonsense is marked by six fundamental weaknesses: poor grammar; inadequate vocabulary; the manufacture of unnecessary words; the random transfer of one part of speech to another; the misapprehension that a portmanteau word must say more than a precise one; and a consequent and incurable delight in abstractions.

There is more to the decline of language than just ignorance and pretence. As I have mentioned, it is international and affects all languages, though none so grievously, I suspect, as English. There is a natural desire among the pretentious to borrow phrases and words from foreign languages (see DISCOURSE), and these, because they are used pretentiously, lend themselves to abuse. To some extent, also, the international nature of the sciences and industry has caused a 'jumbling' of technical terms which have then been borrowed by others. But these are minor components in the international spread of nonsense. I would like to suggest another cause – something much more radical, wholly speculative, quite unprovable, and therefore closely in tune with the modern mind. It is this.

Modern nonsense is merely one aspect of a culture-wide decline that has taken place since the beginning of the century. It is language's attempt to follow art into abstraction, music into atonality, and architecture into cement.

Why is everything modern so frightful? Why are modern buildings ugly and uninhabitable? Why is modern music actively distressing to hear? Why is so much modern art painful or boring to behold?

The modern movement, especially in painting, sculpture, music and architecture, is a fraud. The emperor has no clothes. The language in which his courtiers urge us to marvel at the rich drapery is hollow, inflated, and pretentious. The celebrants of the modern arts are among the worst abusers of English, and it is hard to believe this to be a coincidence.

Nor can it be entirely a coincidence that the art least affected by the modern movement – the one art that cannot retire into abstraction – is the one that has survived and flourished best, against all the predictions and against very long financial odds – the writing of prose.

Unhappily, the misuse of English extends far beyond the arts, and the field of modern nonsense is immense. I have tried to be impartial but it has not been easy, and there will be many to complain that I have not succeeded. There are two glaring omissions in this book. I have omitted all but two or three items of Pentagonese, and I have almost entirely ignored the staggering output of the communist world. I simply did not have space to tackle them, and I thought it better to start at home.

Here I have tried to be fair (see BALANCE). So many entries from business; here an example from advertising; there from critical theory. I thought I had done well until I surveyed the final draft. I now see that merely balancing the sources of my material has done nothing to spare my pet aversions. Readers will identify more of these than I can, but even I can recognise my more obvious *bêtes noires*: modern architecture; post-structuralist critical theory; the caring services; bishops; and all places of education east of a line drawn between Beachy Head and Berwick-upon-Tweed.

I have also invented two categories of person which I then assail without further identification – the modern elect, and the sub-intelligentsia. I could plead that these are merely jocular inventions, for so they are, and that I have no need to elaborate further. But why should I not enjoy myself when the opportunity occurs?

The modern elect – and I chose the word 'elect' deliberately to exploit its pharasaical overtones – embraces: all professional compassion mongers; many Anglican and Catholic Bishops; approximately two-thirds of the teaching profession; all Labour and SLD MPs (and if you think I should include Tories, reflect on the meanings of modern and elect); all vicars who decorate their churches with placards and hold unisex love-ins in the crypt; socialist peers; successful modern architects; TV personalities who espouse causes; all who hold simultaneously the freehold of a Georgian house and socialist principles; every member of the Anglican hierarchy instrumental in ditching the Authorised Version and the Book of Common Prayer; and all socialist ex-ministers who have private incomes, use private medicine, and/or send their children to private schools.

All such people are saying, in one way or another: 'God, I thank thee, that I am not as other men are.'

The sub-intelligentsia provides the helots to the Spartans of the modern elect. It comprises, roughly: all who pay serious attention to the writings, speeches, sermons and other utterances of the foregoing group; all readers of the *Guardian*, *Tribune*, *Marxism Today*, *Spare Rib*, and *New Society*: employees of the caring services; and all writers on sociological, economic, critical and neo-theological themes.

I hear a cry of protest. 'But we're GOOD! What about all those villainous profiteers and arms dealers? They use nonsense too, and they're BAD!'

They are. But they're obviously bad. Commerce and industry do indeed throw up a huge dust cloud of nonsense, and both are plentifully represented in these pages. The business 'nonsenseers' are the kings of pomposity, but their motives are obvious. The lust for gold is difficult to hide, and it is in any case a power substitute, and therefore a more innocent pursuit than the pursuit of power itself. For these reasons, business nonsense, though often of inspired frightfulness, lacks the element of spiritual arrogance that gives the left and its hangers-on the lead.

As I review this typescript, I am a little surprised at its tone of sustained spleen. I attribute it to my annoyance at having to read so much disagreeable matter. The delight to be found in words – even very silly ones – hardly comes across at all. Indeed, here and there I have only just avoided falling into the very frame of mind I castigated at the outset – earnestness.

Never mind. At least I have preserved the Spirit of the Offensive. Not even Lord Cardigan could have cried 'Charge! Charge! Hurrah!' more recklessly, and no-one can deny that we confront an enemy at least as dangerous to the Queen's English as ever the Russian guns were to her light cavalry.

I think I have offended everybody. I have spoken lightly of the Bauhaus. I have mocked 'kids in care'. I have intimated that bankers are tradesmen; that brokers are blockheads. I have blackguarded bishops – archbishops too. I have slighted cement.

I do not pretend that anything I have written will cure the disease afflicting language. A long-term cure lies in areas outside our control: the resumption of teaching in schools; the death penalty for practising sociologists; cold steel. All would help.

In the meantime, however, we can divert ourselves by blowing resounding raspberries at the speech and writing of –

the moderns.

Patrick Scrivenor
March, 1989.

A

**ABOVE-THE-LINE/
BELOW-THE-LINE**

adjective. Advertisers have not been visited by any great law-giver. There has been no Marquess of Queensberry to lay down the rules for them. They hit out wildly, therefore, both ABOVE and BELOW THE LINE, and, what is more, wear no protective devices.

Roughly speaking, ABOVE-THE-LINE ADVERTISING is found in the national papers, in magazines, and on television. BELOW-THE-LINE ADVERTISING is found at the POINT OF SALE. The line is notional, and nothing like so well defined as the belt in boxing. But the jargonauts of ADVERTISING are a merry crew, and crossing the line involves no humiliating or degrading experiences worse than those normal to the trade of copywriting.

ABUSE

noun and *verb.* ABUSE has erupted from its coy bridgehead in the phrase self ABUSE, has by-passed its general meaning of rudeness in speech, and has romped through the language claiming victims left and right. It is now possible to ABUSE practically anything: drink, drugs, dogs, glue, solvent, and children – especially children (see CHILD ABUSE).

> ' ...Newham Monitoring Project is here to help you if you have been racially attacked on the street, at school, at home or racially ABUSED.' (Advertisement in *Spare Rib*, January 1988)

' ... if you think your rights have been ABUSED by the police, or if you have been racially ABUSED or assaulted by the police ...' (*Ibid.*)

Is 'racial ABUSE' just plain old-fashioned rudeness in speech, or something more recondite? How does racial attack differ from ordinary attack? The ABUSE of one's RIGHTS, presumably, goes far beyond abusive speech. The interesting feature of these extracts is the adoption of the word ABUSE to cover any behaviour in another that injures oneself in any way, from genuine injury down to loss of self-esteem.

ACCESSIBLE

adjective. Used contemptuously of writing which makes sense, painting with at least a small figurative element, and music which is not wholly cacophonous. ACCESSIBLE ART is not far off being BLAND.

Curiously enough, no amount of accessibility can make MODERN MUSIC endurable. If it is not ear-shatteringly atonal, it is always like the soundtrack of a B movie.

ACTIVE-SERVICE UNIT

noun. Two or three junior terrorists, blackmailed and coerced by senior terrorists into taking some form of hit-and-run action in which their own risk is minimised, and the risk to passers-by maximised.

'The IRA last night admitted that the three were members of one of its "ACTIVE-SERVICE UNITS", all from West Belfast. A statement said that contrary to reports from Gibraltar of a shoot-out, none of the three were [*sic*] armed "so there could have been no gun battle".' (Report in the *Independent*, 7.3.88.)

It took the Irish to invent the unarmed ACTIVE-SERVICE UNIT.

ACTIVIST   *noun*. Trouble-maker.

ACUPUNCTURE   *noun*. In ancient China doctors were paid only while their patients were well. As soon as they fell ill, payment ceased. The doctors therefore devised a mildly painful and obviously ineffective treatment whose sole object was to discourage patients from consulting them.

ADDITIVES   *noun*. The raw materials of FOOD SOPHISTICATION. Elements added to food:

(a) to make it last longer;
(b) to make it less disgusting;
(c) to lend it an appearance conforming with urban notions of what dead animal and vegetable matter should look like.

ADDITIVES have made a tremendous contribution to medical science by triggering the growth of a whole new medical industry – the allergy industry. They are anathema to the ENVIRON-MENTALLY and ORGANICALLY conscious, who, without them, would scarcely have anything to talk about. They are categorised by letters, and 'E ADDITIVES' are the ones to look out for.

But all ADDITIVES are very wicked.

ADJUST   *verb*. To alter something to one's advantage without blatant falsification. The high euphemistic value of ADJUST lies in the smallness of the alteration implied, and in echoes of 'just' in the sense of 'fair'.

Together they convey a sense of precise and justified change. The 'seasonal adjustment' of government figures has disquieting reminders of cooking: 'ADJUST seasoning to taste.'

ADVERSE COST IMPLICATIONS

noun. Having to pay more, or even having to pay at all.

'Despite the mistake it is already clear that the submarine will be delivered on time and with no ADVERSE COST IMPLICATIONS for the Ministry of Defence.' (Rodney Leach, Chairman and CHIEF EXECUTIVE of Vickers Shipbuilding, writing in *The Times*, 14.4.88)

This means – 'We won't charge the Navy more for our mistake'. But it is clear that all pricing is a form of ADVERSE COST IMPLICATION. 'Price' is a harsh, customer-negative word, and must be eliminated.

How much better if a manufacturer were to say 'The ADVERSE COST IMPLICATION of the new wash-dry in-home laundressette is a mere £999.95p plus VAT.'

ADVERTISING

noun. A pot of message.

To 'advertise', from the French *avertir* and Latin *advertere*, means to inform. In its modern usage it covers a comprehensive range of misinformation (see DISINFORMATION), often beguilingly deployed.

Like all forms of dishonest persuasion, ADVERTISING follows the law of diminishing returns. The cleverer you are, the cleverer you have to be next time to achieve the same effect.

AESTHETIC

adjective. An ugly word which, naturally, means 'pertaining to the appreciation or criticism of the beautiful'. It is a pretentious word, but at least it has a proper meaning. The 'ic' ending attracts the moderns like wasps to a jam-pot and, with SEMANTICS and DIALECTIC, AESTHETIC is widely used as a noun. It is in this capacity that it plumbs its full usefulness as a piece of nonsense, in phrases like 'the Bauhaus AESTHETIC' or 'the dust-bin-lid AESTHETIC'.

'Stripped to essentials, this collection of furniture, drawings and sculpture from the University of East Anglia commemorates the streamlined AESTHETIC of the Bauhaus ...' (Allen Robertson, *Time Out*, 3.2.88)

'Style' would be more straightforward than AESTHETIC in this context, but much less exciting.

AFFIRMATIVE

adjective. The opposite of NEGATIVE, but less widely misused, perhaps because the opponents of the moderns are more often NEGATIVE than AFFIRMATIVE. Here it seems to mean 'confirming or reinforcing'.

'Well before Foucault, Gramsci had grasped the idea that culture serves authority, and ultimately the national State, not because it represses and coerces, but because it is AFFIRMATIVE, positive and persuasive.' (Edward Said, *The World, the Text and the Critic*, Cambridge, 1983).

Being translated, this means: 'A number of people – too many to ignore – actually likes traditional paintings, plays, books, buildings, sculpture and music. Rather more, in fact, than like the modern versions. This is politically intolerable to us, the moderns. Therefore traditional culture is a conspiracy to enslave these people to the State.'

AFFIRMATIVE ACTION
noun. Usually sitting in a public place to annoy the police – in other words, negative inaction.

ALPHANUMERIC
adjective. Computerese for 'combining letters, numbers, and symbols. A FACILITY frequently to be found in ty*!wr¾t$%s, WORD PROCESSORS, and c'mp#t›rs.

AMBASSADOR-FOR-THE-SPORT
noun. A SPORTSMAN who is not, for the moment, drunk, drugged or menacing in his demeanour.

AMBIDEXTROUS
adjective Sexually disoriented. Used, by false analogy with its correct meaning of 'having equal skill with both hands', to mean 'having equal relish for both sexes'. The expression AC/DC is used to indicate the same mishap, possibly in an attempt to suggest the shocking excitements of high voltage.

AMENITY
noun. A word now so generalised that it indicates anything that can possibly be described as a public convenience.

AMENITY is a favourite with estate agents, and they use it to cover any not-actually-lethal feature of a property's surroundings. Things as diverse as a bus stop and a swimming pool are referred to as AMENITIES.

AMERICAN CONSTITUTION

noun. A very faulty document hastily flung together by a dissident set of slave owners and tobacco growers, who recoiled from the prospect of having to make a contribution to the cost of their defence against the French.

The colonists made an attempt to incorporate the subtleties of the British constitution, but did not really understand them. For instance, rushing headlong to embrace the notion of a division of powers, they imagined, in their excessive way, that the more powers they divided the better. As a result, the Executive, Legislature and Judiciary are overburdened with wholly unnecessary powers, and constantly hamper one another in the exercise of their duties (see JUDICIAL ACTIVIST). The head of state and the head of the executive are the same person. Fatal. The Legislature and the Executive are elected separately, and often at odds. Key posts in the Judiciary change with the administration. The whole thing's a shambles. What they most lack, but have never been able to admit, is a permanent, unelected head of state – in other words a monarch.

The slaves cropped up again, too.

ANALOGUE (American **ANALOG**)

1. *adjective*, as in ANALOGUE computer. A computer which operates by differentiating between differentials. Need more be said? It is distinct from a digital computer, which counts on its fingers.

2. *Noun.* ANALOGUE, analogy, and analogous, are great favourites with the moderns, who love their quasi-scientific sound and scatter them about like a berserk pheasant-shooter scattering lead. Analogy means a similarity of attributes, analogous

means having such a similarity, and ANALOGUE means an analogous word or thing. These distinctions were never absolute, and analogy is usually employed as a less obscure synonym for ANALOGUE.

All three words have specialised meanings in mathematics and zoology, and since there are simpler everyday equivalents, it would seem fair to reserve the longer words for specialised use. But it is too much to hope.

'The ANALOG for the satisfaction of wants for collective goods is not an equivalent process of private maximization in a market process in which the parameters have been adjusted to reflect these collective wants. That is the modern Liberal heresy.' (Professor Fred Hirsch, *Social Limits to Growth*, Routledge and Kegan Paul, London, 1977)

A possible rendering of this bewildering sentence could be: 'Achieving the maximum private involvement in the market is not the same as satisfying the need for collective goods, even though the market largely reflects society's collective needs.' I'm not sure. But notice how deploying the word ANALOG immediately threw the sentence off the rails. The repeated 'fors' and 'ins'. The main verb lost amid the attendant cohorts of clauses. The obligatory modernisms 'process' and 'parameters'. (See DISTRIBUTIONAL COMPULSION and POSITIONAL GOODS.)

ANTIQUE

noun. An ANTIQUE used to be a work of art or artefact more than 100 years old, but the word has marched forward and now it means anything of any age that is second hand (see PRE-OWNED). It sometimes includes brand new artefacts of a certain style.

> 'ANTIQUES old and new'. (A sign displayed in a shop window in Massachusetts, USA)

ANTIQUE is also used as a verb: to ANTIQUE. This is the overt activity which, in its covert form, is called 'distressing' – simulating an ANTIQUE appearance in new furniture by spilling things on it, bashing it with hammers, and making woodworm holes by firing number 9 shot out of a sawn-off shotgun.

To ANTIQUE furniture is normally an honest, if misguided, act of reproduction. 'Distressing' is almost always faking.

APARTHEID   *noun.* An elaborate system of segregation which the Boers have found to be the only means of distinguishing themselves from their fellow Africans. (See PLURAL RELATIONS.)

APPROPRIATE   *verb.* Misappropriate.

APOLITICISM   *noun.* The condition of being right wing. 'If you are not with us, you are against us,' chant the left, and therefore anyone who indulges in the imposture of political neutrality is a hideous FASCIST. (See INDIRECT RACISM.)

> A work of ART that is COMMITTED strips the magic from a work of ART that is content to be a fetish, an idle pastime for those who would like to sleep through the deluge that threatens them, in an APOLITICISM that is in fact deeply political.' (Theodor Adorno,

'COMMITMENT', *Aesthetics and Politics*, London, 1977)

It hasn't occurred to Mr Adorno that to sleep through a deluge is almost certainly the best way of coping with it.

ARCHITECT

noun. A destroyer of cities, a vandal. ARCHITECTS have succeeded where the Luftwaffe failed, and have destroyed more British cities than Herr Heinkel ever dreamed of. As jolly old Hermann Goering himself might have remarked: 'When I hear the word ARCHITECT I reach for my revolver.' (This passage was written before the Prince of Wales made the same analogy in a public speech. I see no reason to abandon it. Great minds think alike.)

'Decorative ART is dead. Modern town PLANNING comes to birth with a new ARCHITECTURE. By this immense step of evolution, so brutal and overwhelming, we burn our bridges and break with the past.' (Charles Edouard Jeanneret, otherwise known as le Corbusier, *The City of Tomorrow*, 1924)

The Swiss have inflicted three exceptional barbarities on the world – the cuckoo-clock, the yodel, and le Corbusier. Even they are so ashamed of the last that they have managed to pass him off as French.

Corbusier is one of the great founding fathers of Modern Nonsense. It is difficult to know where to start, but we cannot complain that we were not warned. The words 'brutal and overwhelming' are Corbusier's own.

History wisely separated the English from their continental neighbours by language as well as by geography. Until recently this has had the great advantage of protecting us from baneful influences, but it has also had the disadvantage of generating respect at a distance. Most Englishmen nourish a secret suspicion that the Europeans are in some way more intellectually gifted than the English. What a shattering moment of disillusion awaits the Englishman who opens the pages of the father of modern ARCHITECTURE.

As a writer, le Corbusier falls into the category of the 'declamatory waffler', and in his more excitable moments is capable of great absurdity:

> 'The circulation of traffic demands the straight line.' (*Ibid.*)

The line, sinuous or straight, seems to stimulate him to frenzy:

> 'But when the line is continuous and regular, and the forms are full and rounded without a break, and governed by a clear guiding rule, then the senses are solaced, the mind is ravished, liberated, lifted out of chaos and flooded with light. The word "mastery" comes to the mind, it glows brightly and we are happy. Here is our true basis; a physiological and irrefutable one. A city can overhelm us with its broken lines; the sky is torn by its ragged outline. Where shall we find repose?' (*Ibid.*)

Are these the utterances of one of the '*plus logiques gens du monde*', if only by adoption? And how we now long for the ragged outline!

To be fair to the French, they would have nothing to do with Corbusier's plan to redesign Paris, and, compared with England, France has remained unspoilt by

Corbusier's heirs and assigns. This is what the French escaped.

'The Voisin scheme for Paris means regaining possession of the eternal centre of the city. ... This plan makes a frontal attack on the most diseased quarters of the city, and the narrowest streets ... its aim is rather to open up in the strategic heart of Paris a splendid system of communication. As against streets ranging from 20 to 35 feet in width with cross roads every 20, 30 or 50 yards, its aim is to establish a plan of the 'gridiron' system with roads 150, 250 to 400 feet in width, with cross roads every 350 or 400 yards. And on the vast island sites thus formed to build immense cruciform sky scrapers, so creating a vertical city, a city which will pile up the cells which have for so long been crushed on the ground, and set them on high above the earth, bathed in light and air.' (*Ibid.*)

There is an accompanying sketch which should give all who love Paris cause for deep relief. Corbusier was well aware of the damage he would be doing, and allowed himself to indulge in silly little mock heroics about it.

'My scheme is brutal, because town existence and life itself are brutal: life is pitiless, it must defend itself, hemmed in as it is on all sides by death. To overcome death, constant activity is necessary.' (*Ibid.*)

This is little short of demented, but among the modern elect Corbusier's writings enjoy the status of Holy Writ, more even than his buildings, which are mercifully few. At heart Corbusier was not an architect at all, but an engineer. He was obsessed with machines, and did not seem to like buildings as buildings at all. They are, in his famous phrase:

'Machines for living in'.

The anology is, of course, quite false. Machines consume energy to perform a task. Buildings provide accommodation, meeting places, places to work. They may have machines in them that perform tasks relevant to the purpose of the building, but that is as far as you can go.

But Corbusier was really quite besotted with machines. Here he goes again:

'Machinery has projected us into a new epoch.'

He may not have noticed it, but we move into new epochs all the time, with or without the help of machinery.

'The street is a traffic machine ...'

And:

'The river is a kind of liquid railway.'

'A town is a tool.'

In all this he was a very characteristic modern. The pompous phrase-making. The spurious populism. The constant borrowings from other disciplines to create an impression of omniscience. But he was also a relentless polemicist, often more interested in scoring points than making them. The frontispiece of *The City of Tomorrow* is an aerial photograph of a London suburb. The caption reads:

'The town spread out over an immense area. Narrow "corridor" streets. Back gardens that are little more than yards.'

The streets in the picture are not particularly narrow. The gardens seem to be at least forty or fifty feet long. The irony is that these not-very-inviting properties are now hugely valuable, partly because no-one can bear to live in the 'cells', 'units', and 'volumes playing about in space' constructed by Corbusier's followers.

The picture is especially relevant, because it is Britain that has suffered most from the attentions of modern ARCHITECTS. Neither language nor geography could save us. Modern ARCHITECTURE came late to Britain, in ignoble but suitable confederacy with socialised PLANNING. Defenders of Corbusier will assert that the barbarities inflicted on London and other British cities were nothing to do with him and do not conform to his plans. To all his plans, thank God, they do not.

There are many passages in Corbusier's books in which he praises the architecture of the past, and holds up New York and Chicago as aberrations. But his praise is lip service, and given only to old buildings that conform to a grid pattern, like the Place des Vosges in Paris. Venice, for instance, he can't be doing with at all, except for the Procuraties, and he is in two minds even about them. As for his strictures on the American skyscrapers, rarely can pot and kettle have been in such close chromatic harmony. The plans and elevations of his proposed cities bear a close resemblance to what has been done in Britain, and, with the experience we now have, we can see that they would have been inhuman and uninhabitable places.

Nor do I think it fanciful to suggest that their inhumanity could have been deduced at the time from Corbusier's terminology:

' ... the majestic rhythm of vertical surfaces receding into the distance in a

noble perspective and outlining pure
forms. From one skyscraper to another a
relationship of voids and solids is
established.'

This is very advanced Nonsense, and it
should be clear that nothing intelligent,
useful or good to look at could possibly
proceed from a mind so taken up with
abstractions.

It is odd that the Swiss should live in such
a beautiful country, and happily destroy
the beauty with all the paraphernalia of ski
tourism. Corbusier was a Swiss to the last
rectangle on his plans. Hygiene ('bathing in
light'), and order (all those straight lines)
were absolutely essential to him. Any hint
of disorder drove him frantic.

' ... our eyes, on the contrary, are subject
to the limitations of their visual field,
and can only see cell after cell; and the
sight of these provides a jagged loose,
diversified, multiplied and nerve-
wracking spectacle; the sky is seen
against a ragged outline and each house
suggests, even by its very shape, some
different order of thing. The eye is
overwhelmed, tired, and hurt ...'

In spite of writing screeds of this sort of
nonsense, Corbusier has had a dramatic
effect on his fellow architects. The machine
analogy has caught on and stuck. And in
spite of a healthy reaction, both inside the
profession and without, there are still
plenty of heroic moderns about, justifying
their horrible misdeeds with rubbish
similar to that quoted above.

But no spoken or written excuses will
avail. All that is needed is to stand on
Greenwich hill and look out over London.
In the foreground are three great works of
traditional architecture: Wren's Hospital,

Inigo Jones's Queen's House, and Wren's Observatory. Now raise your eyes and look beyond the river. What you see is a wholescale tragedy. Tawdry, ugly blocks thrust themselves up everywhere. 'Volumes playing about in space' there are in abundance. 'Units' and 'cells' in plenty. 'Voids' and 'solids' relating all over the place. The National Westminster building, the Post Office Tower, all are the hideous, monstrous offspring of Corbusier's half-baked intellect and absurd preoccupations. But the contrast with Wren and Jones is too great. The moderns are found wanting.

ARCHITECTURE

noun. The internal design and structure of a computer system. Computerists reserve this term for the abstract design of the system, rather than the crude nuts and bolts of the HARDWARE. Why they should want to borrow the name of the most debased and decadent of all the modern ARTS is known only to themselves. It is like a young acolyte taking the name of a defrocked cleric.

> 'The ARCHITECTURE of IBM's Early Computers ... The first chapter of this commemorative issue is devoted to the subject of computer systems ARCHITECTURE and development.' (*IBM Journal of Research and Development*, September, 1981)

The title has all the proud ring of 'Early Byzantine ARCHITECTURE'. Note that it is not a computer that has ARCHITECTURE, but a 'system'. Note also that the 's' on the end of 'systems' has no apostrophe. We are offered three nouns in a row each qualifying the next, with the result that the whole sentence – which begins, if not promisingly, at any rate comprehensibly – degenerates into a clogged mass of syllables whose meaning has to be extracted by force. Why not: 'The first chapter of this commemorative issue deals with the development of computer systems'?

ARMY COUNCIL   *collective noun.* A group of senior terrorists who issue communiqués explaining the DIALECTICAL significance of the atrocities committed by their juniors.

ART   *noun.* A word used by frauds to frighten the laity. Everyone knows that ART exists, and that it deserves reverence. Any person defective in reverence is a Philistine, or, worst of all, middle class. Terror of falling into these despised categories serves to stifle all criticism, and a wide range of rubbish is consequently passed off as ART, which is now no more than the generic name for any truly unproductive process.

> 'This is gallery ART with a vengeance, as much to do with the space around objects as the objects themselves.' (Stuart Morgan, 'Degree Zero, Grenville Davey', a contribution to *artscribe*, January 1988)

Grenville Davey belongs to what you might call the bog-seat school of ART. He specialises in domestic or domestic-looking artefacts – towel rails, shaving mirrors, manhole covers – placed in isolation, and of such breathtaking banality that the space around them really does take on a certain allure.

ART DEALER/ ANTIQUE DEALER   *noun.* A cynic who knows the price of what he wants to sell to you, and the value of what you want to sell to him.

ARTWORK *noun.* The antithesis of a work of ART.

> 'Bellemare makes a deliberately sub-textual reading of his chosen ARTWORKS ...' (John Miller, 'Stations', a contribution to *artscribe*, January 1988)

A sub-textual reading is, presumably, reading below the lines. And Mr Bellemare is, apparently, well equipped for this difficult feat. Two sentences before the above extract Mr Miller explains Mr Bellemare's ordered approach to his texts:

> 'Roger Bellemare is more explicit in his thematic exegesis. His INSTALLATION unfolds sequentially.' (*Ibid.*)

One gets very little idea from all this what Roger Bellemare's ARTWORKS actually look like. Mr Bellemare chose fourteen ARTWORKS to represent the Stations of the Cross, installed them sequentially, and Bingo! Rapture! Or rapture for Mr Miller, who gets the opportunity to air at great length his views on religion ('Our grasp of religion must be thoroughly historicized'); ART gallery administration ('This kind of curatorial intervention implicitly challenges the supposed autonomy of the artist'); and on his own eclectic learning ('Here the films of Pasolini in their dialectical comprehension of the classic texts of Aeschylus, Chaucer and D.A.F.Sade – not to mention the Book of Matthew – stand in stark opposition to the foregoing'). Well yes. The Book of Matthew – quite.

Only after this does he get down to a discussion of the ARTWORKS themselves, and then sketchily. But, in modern ART criticism, the eye is less important than a grasp of the jargon of the sub-intelligentsia.

The Design community also use ARTWORK for any 'camera ready' material mounted on board or stiff paper. Usually there is little work involved and less ART. (See DESIGNER.)

ASSERTIVENESS THEORY

noun. A branch of SOCIAL SCIENCE by which sociologists hope to exalt the humble and meek.

ASYLUM

noun. The source of an unhappy misunderstanding. The Soviet authorities, fired by the humane notion of Political ASYLUM, mistakenly developed the practice of popping their dissidents into loony bins.

AT RISK

adjective. 1. What you are if you're not in care.

2. The description of any KID stranded in the howling wilderness beyond the pale of the social services.

3. The precarious situation of all children left to the tender mercies of their parents, against whose universal predisposition to CHILD ABUSE the CARING services struggle night and day.

ATTENTION SPAN

noun. A term used by educationalists to indicate the brief interval during which the average teacher can distract the average child from its natural interest in violence, theft, and unrestrained exercise of the ego. (See EDUCATION.)

ATTITUDINAL

adjective. Having attitudes uncongenial to a social worker, and thereby creating a 'hostile ATTITUDINAL ENVIRONMENT' in which his or her 'clients' droop and wither away.

'Attitude' as a noun is a vague enough word. ATTITUDINAL is vaguer still, giving no hint as to which of 'attitude's' meanings is being used adjectively. Linked to ENVIRONMENT it becomes meaningless.

'Attitude' can mean 'position', but there is no hope that 'positional' (see POSITIONAL GOODS) will yield a clue to ATTITUDINAL.

'Positional' is gritty, economic, and meaningless. ATTITUDINAL is wet, sociological and meaningless. A 'hostile ATTITUDINAL ENVIRONMENT' is merely the manners and behaviour of all those who do not subordinate every moment of their time to the interests of the DISADVANTAGED.

AUTHENTIC

adjective. A more resounding synonym for real, actual or genuine. Never believe the claim that anything offered for sale is AUTHENTIC.

> 'An AUTHENTIC Italian restaurant where no-one's been shot ... yet.' (Advertisement for the Park Avenue restaurant Positano, 1987)

I know of several Italian restaurants which could be made more AUTHENTIC by shooting the chef, and perhaps the owner of this 'eaterie' is seeking an improvement along these lines. For a long time everyone, including the New Yorkers themselves, has been at pains to emphasise that all New Yorkers suffer from infantilism, but surely not so badly as to respond to this advertisment.

It was riddled with simulated, non-AUTHENTIC bullet holes.

AUTHORED

verb, past participle. Wrote or written. 'He AUTHORED'; 'the book was

AUTHORED by'. An unnecessary verb manufactured from the noun 'author'. A piece of *Time – Life* or *Readers' Digest* house style. It is difficult to plumb the mind that decided to replace 'written' or 'wrote' with AUTHORED. Sometimes, turning the pages of American periodicals, one is left with a strong feeling that their ghastly, cheery style is a piece of buffoonery; an elaborate self-parody. But the citizens of the great republic don't pay good dollars for buffoonery. These publications are taken seriously, and are widely read. Their style is accepted as good, no-nonsense, plain-talking English.

Like all the worst aspects of American life – why can't we get Californian wines as readily as Californian jargon? – AUTHORED has made its way across the pond. Here is an example of the word-craft of one who AUTHORS for *The Times*:

'... an enquiry is necessary to answer questions raised by Mr Peter Wright, the former MI5 officer who AUTHORED *Spycatcher*.' (Report in *The Times*, 17.10.88)

Milton! Thou shouldst be living at this hour: *The Times* hath need of thee; it is a fen of stagnant authors.

AVANT-GARDE   *noun*. Those in the van of MODERNISM, especially in the ARTS.

'Thus, in recent years, when POST-MODERNISTS proposed a redefined theoretical framework for the production and reception of ART, many of the tenets of the AVANT-GARDE as originally conceived within MODERN-ISM no longer seemed VIABLE or relevant.' (Brian Wallis, reviewing the book *The Transformation of the*

AVANT-GARDE, in *Art in America,* February 1988).

This sentence is not wholly nonsense, since its meaning can be discovered without undue labour, but it contains so many of the key ART crit words that I couldn't resist it. Notice how nothing can happen without 'a redefined theoretical framework'. In the old days pictures got painted in the hope that some patron would buy them. Now there must be a theoretical framework, without which no-one can summon up the confidence to apply paint to flat surface. ART is no longer painted or sculpted: it is no longer seen or beheld. It is 'produced' and 'received'. Unviable tenets are rejected; new ones embraced.

The lay observer is bound to ask at some point 'Where and what is the ART?' Poor, deluded fool. Benighted BOURGEOIS individualist. Never mind the ART! Feel the theoretical framework.

The AVANT-GARDE has left ART far behind.

AWARENESS *noun.* An affliction of the organs of perception, chronic and incurable. There are many strains of this virus, of which Social AWARENESS is the most unpleasant. To be socially aware causes loss of sight, loss of speech, drooling at the mouth, deafness and incontinence. (See CARING and SUPPORTIVE).

B

BACKLASH

noun. The objections of anyone right-of-centre to the activities of anyone left-of-centre.

BACKWARDATION

noun. Loss. A very undesirable state of affairs that sometimes arises on the commodity exchange, when what you have just bought is already worth less than what you paid for it. This is BACKWARDATION, or a disadvantageous difference between the 'spot price' and the 'forward price'. An *advantageous* difference is another matter altogether and is called profit, or sometimes, bafflingly, 'contango'.

BALANCE

noun. A drastically simplified method – adapted to the needs of broadcasting – of approaching the truth by representing only the two most extreme views of a matter.

BALANCE OF PAYMENTS

noun. A rare moment of national equipoise on the seesaw of international default.

BALANCE OF PAYMENTS is most often used to indicate a drastic imbalance. In Britain, it means 'We're still importing far more than we export.'

BALL GAME

noun. A perplexing North American sport, which is always 'whole new'.

BALL PARK FIGURE

noun. An imaginary figure. A modest guess. To hit a home run in baseball involves smiting the ball out of the park. A score

31

within the park, therefore, is a more modest score. Hence a BALL PARK FIGURE – a modest fiction, pitched low to encourage belief.

This is a very useful, USER FRIENDLY term for moments of crisis in the board room. When asked to estimate the year's likely losses, the hard-pressed financial secretary can say: 'Well, at a BALL PARK FIGURE, about £2m', knowing full well that even £3m would be well within the park.

BANK

noun. An institution which fulfills its obligation to safeguard your money by frustrating your access to it.

Bankers need your money to play with. Behind their sober suitings and High Street facades they are desperate, bulging-eyed addicts, hooked on the one-armed bandit of finance. There is no substance to their business; no bars of gold in the vaults. Their wealth is represented solely by their dexterity in the management of money.

Your money.

BAR

noun. A place where most men spend money, but where publicans and barristers make it.

BARRISTER

noun. An unusual, perverse, and odd person who needs to be called to the bar.

As users of language BARRISTERS occupy a curious position. From time to time they are called upon to use language with extraordinary precision, but for the day-to-day purposes of courtroom histrionics they have evolved a strange school of euphemnism.

'As your Lordship pleases' means 'Senile buffoon'.

'I put it to you that ...' means 'For what I am about to say I have no evidence, but if I suggest it unpleasantly enough it may find a toehold in the granite craniums of the jury.'

'I object' means 'Unless I interrupt immediately facts highly prejudicial to my client will be disclosed.'

BEHAVIOURAL ENRICHMENT *noun.* The art of making entertainment for animals kept in captivity. The reverse of the chimpanzees' tea party.

' ... [to appoint] an entertainments officer to devise ways of keeping the inhabitants of London Zoo amused and stimulated. His actual title is BEHAVIOURAL ENRICHMENT Research Fellow ...' (A report by John Young in *The Times*, 15.2.88)

The new Research Fellow is to develop 'devices to ENRICH the animals' ENVIRONMENT and to reduce abnormal behaviour associated with captivity'. To this end he will provide self-operated showers for pigs and apes, fun ways of getting food for everything from stick insects to Siberian wolves, and a musical keyboard for the orang-utans.

I predict that this initiative will fall foul of one of mankind's most peristent misapprehensions – the conviction that animals are less intelligent than men. Animals, of course, are far more intelligent than men, and for the very reason that is usually advanced for being less intelligent. Their brains are much smaller. No animal's brain is equipped to be preoccupied with the irrelevancies that vex and distract mankind, and they are able to devote their entire intellectual energy to what really matters – food, sleep, and sex. No-one who keeps domestic animals, or who spends much time close to wild animals, can fail to note the skill with which they always get what they want.

I further predict that in less than three years one slightly-used Research fellow will be carted discreetly away hatch-wards, gibbering and sticking straws in his hair. They'll get him. You see.

BELIEF

noun. A condition of inflamed egoism, in which figments of the sufferer's imagination are exalted to the status of absolute truth. (see BUDDHISM, CHRISTIANITY, HINDUISM, ISLAM and JUDAISM).

BEST SELLER

noun. Any book of which not more than half the copies remain unsold.

BIG BANG

noun. A colloquial name given to the theory that the universe originated in an explosion. Of what? you may ask. In 1986, the term was borrowed by the financial community to lend cosmic significance to the dull events that overtook them in that year. These happenings, otherwise called DEREGULATION, were designed to clean up a notoriously raffish quarter of the City of London – The Floor – by luring the footpads and cutpurses who used to be its habitués into brand new, electronic surroundings where they were able to shout and gesticulate at machines instead of each other. As remedial therapy this plan has not worked, but at least it has got them out of the public eye.

BIKINI AREA

noun. The female crutch. In 1987 an advertisement appeared on London's underground trains for 'Bikini Bare

Depilatory Cream'. Coyly mooted as the 'Bare Essential', it was recommended for use with 'the new hi-thigh swimsuits'. The product's painless qualities were strongly emphasised, and the final, clinching recommendation was the calm reassurance 'no razor stubble'. The whole advertisement was a masterpiece of prurient euphemism, revealing, not the hand of an inspired humourist, but the struggles of a desperate hack caught between the upper millstone of THE PRODUCT, and the nether millstone of the Advertising Standards Authority.

BIOSPHERE OVERLOAD

noun. Us; and too many of us. Or rather the consequences of too many of us. The term 'demographic strain' is a gentler way of drawing our attention to our superfluity to the planet's needs.

BIRTHDAY HONOURS (NEW YEAR HONOURS, DISSOLUTION HONOURS, ETC)

noun. The British, in their frivolous way, have perfected a system of drawing attention to the truly dishonourable by honouring them. They have devised a scale of titles and dignities which they heap on all those who have fawned, flattered, fought, kicked and stabbed their way to the top. It is an uniquely impartial system, showing no favour. POLITICIANS, businessmen, trade unionists, ARCHITECTS, entrepreneurs in the 'arts', popular singers, SPORTSMEN, traitors — all, and many more, are in due course branded with the mark of infamy, as damning as threadbare trouser knees, or a brown tongue.

BLACK

adjective. Brown.

'Trainer Skills for Young BLACK Professionals ...

This is a positive action training programme run by ITS for MSC and we welcome applications from BLACK people regardless of sex or disability.' (Action for Jobs advertisement in *New Society*, 22.1.88).

It is against the law in Britain to discriminate on grounds of race, but you would be wrong if you thought this advertisement breaks the law. This is not RACIAL DISCRIMINATION but POSITIVE DISCRIMINATION, and not only legal but devoutly to be wished.

But BLACK people are not BLACK. No more are white people white. Europeans are a sort of sallow pink, and negroes are a rich chocolate brown. If we used the terms 'brown' and 'pink' instead of the loaded and inaccurate terms 'BLACK' and 'white', we would quickly see how ridiculous all the fuss is.

But it would cause difficulty for the sponsors of this advertisement because Indians and other Asians are also brown, and they are clearly not included on this 'positive action' bandwagon, being generally supposed to be less in need of POSITIVE DISCRIMINATION.

BLAND

adjective. A term of derision employed by the ART mafia. Anything that falls short of their high standards of ugliness, irrelevance and incomprehensibility, is BLAND. (See ACCESSIBLE.)

BLOCK STUDIES

noun. A BLOCK is a number of UNITS. No wiser? BLOCK STUDIES are part of an 'integrated teaching system'. Getting warmer? A number of BLOCKS might make up a 'course' foundation, intermediate or advanced. Give up?

To fall into the hands of educationalists no longer means attending lessons, passing examinations, and learning something. No, no. You master each unit, assemble them in BLOCKS, and build up your coursework.

It's very like elementary bricklaying, but less difficult.

BLOCK VOTE

noun. An ingenious system of multiplication, which puts the sheen of democracy on the lacklustre of oligarchy by spuriously representing one vote as several million.

BLUE CHIP

adjective. Posh, exclusive, UP-MARKET, PRESTIGIOUS.

'Corporate/BLUE CHIP Accounts: Account Executive: Applicants for this position will ideally have some PR consultancy experience, handling appropriate accounts. More importantly however, you will have acquired good marketing/corporate-planning experience, leading to a strong commercial AWARENESS.' (Advertisement placed in *The Times*, 18.11.87, by Applied Management Services Ltd)

Those involved in the Tombola of staff recruitment feel their chances in the lucky dip are improved if they carry the battle into the enemy's camp, and sternly admonish potential applicants that they 'will' have certain qualifications. Note the dextrous opening of the second sentence – 'More importantly however'. I like that.

The advertisement goes on 'You will have a high academic background (Graduate level) with excellent presentation ...'. Why not 'You will have a degree, and be well turned out' or 'of good appearance'?

BODY-GUILT   *noun.* 'Nudespeak' (see NATURISM) for what you suffer from if it is not your immediate impulse to take off your clothes, even in the bracing latitudes of the British Isles.

> 'Walk upstream SW where trees and solitude encourage an ablution as practised in the years when BODY-GUILT was less since the wearing of costumes was unknown. We can see in paintings of Brighton and Scarborough that mixed nude bathing was quite normal at the latter end of the eighteenth century.' (Entry in *Inland Free Sun*, a guide to Naturist sites, by Phil Vallack, 1988)

I doubt very much whether any mixed nude bathing in the eighteenth century went unattended by BODY-GUILT of the most exravagant and elaborate kind.

BONK   *verb.* To BONK is the latest in a very long line of euphemisms for the procreative act. It takes over from coarse and aggressive terms like 'screw' and 'shag', and is on the whole preferable, being cheerful and silly. It enters the realms of nonsense through its adoption by tabloid headline writers, who have at last got a four-letter word meaning Hogmagandie which they can print. BONK suffers by association with 'bonkers', which means daft, mad, or eccentric. Can it be long before we have a film, play or song entitled 'Bonkers about BONKING'?

On the page BONK looks very like 'BANK', and can occasionally figure in illuminating misprints: Merchant BONK, 'don't BONK on it', BONK deposit boxes, and, last but hardly least, The Royal BONK of Scotland.

BORN-AGAIN CHRISTIAN

noun. A used, reconditioned Christian. Not a good bargain. (See CHRISTIANITY.)

BOTTOM LINE SPIN-OFF

noun. An unexpected advantage accruing from the last-ditch phase of any process or operation. Thus the victim of a car accident who discovers at the last moment that flames have a cauterising effect on open wounds, may be said to have enjoyed BOTTOM LINE SPIN-OFF.

BOURGEOIS

noun. A contemptible person of exclusively BLAND tastes.

BRIGADE

noun. Traditionally a grouping of about 3,000 soldiers. In the case of the Irish Republican Army, however, a BRIGADE consists of only three – on the grounds, no doubt, that they are one thousand times more brutal and licentious than any other variety of soldier.

BROAD-BASED

adjective. The characteristic of any institution the range of whose activities is beyond the wit or industry of an economist to explain.

BROAD GAUGE THINKER

noun. Zimri in *Absalom and Achitophel.*

'In the first rank of these did Zimri stand.
A man so various that he seem'd to be
Not one, but all mankind's epitome.
Stiff in opinions, always in the wrong;
Was everything by starts and nothing long: ...'

Dryden's attack on the Duke of Buckingham might just as well be aimed at the many BROAD GAUGE or LATERAL thinkers of our own time.

BUDDHISM   *noun.* A philosophy that deprecates thought and recommends an absolutely mindless condition of cerebral vacuum misleadingly termed 'meditation'. Alone among religions it confronts the central characteristic of them all – escapism – and insolently turns the tables by declaring the material world to be an illusion. Its followers (unlike the founder) are consequently lean and hungry, and frequently beg for illusory money to feed their illusory appetites. Buddhism is the least baneful of the great religions, but has done much harm by encouraging misapprehension about the Lotus Flower.

BUDGET   *noun.* A ceremony, similar to the notional deference paid by Roman emperors to the senate, in which an elected robber tells you how much of your own money you are to be allowed to keep.

BUGGER   *noun.* One who privily and by night plants recording and/or transmitting equipment in an opponent's house or office. Throughout the WATERGATE hearings, British television audiences were diverted by frequent references to what the BUGGERS had or had not done.

BUGGER continues to be widely used as a term of abuse or a general swear word, but in its strict meaning of one addicted to Hunnish malpractices it is on the decline. Such people are now called GAYS.

A few bold spirits, however, still fly the Hunnish flag, even in the post-AIDS era.

'Wilson's pose of urbane sophisticate rarely convinces, undermined as it is by his moralising prurience, misogyny, and a wholly inappropriate naivety (BUGGERING while being BUGGERED is, in fact, neither difficult nor unusual).' (Tim Clark, reviewing Colin Wilson's book, *The Misfits*, in *Time Out*, 3.2.88)

Rarely can such a fatuously self-important sentence have been written.

BUSTED CONVERTIBLE

noun. Not a pranged sports car, but a 'security' called a CONVERTIBLE which has suddenly become terribly insecure by reason of the collapse in price of the underlying equity.

BUZZ WORD

noun. Any word or phrase, including itself, temporarily in vogue among the fatuous.

C

CADRE

noun. In the communist world merely a local executor of the Party's will. In the capitalist world the term becomes much more exciting, denoting a gang of malcontents so power hungry that they will grab even the vestigial traces of power suggested by CADRE's meaning of a 'sleeping' cell of revolutionaries.

CADRE is drawn from the apparently bottomless well of French military terminology, and it means the permanent framework of a regiment; the establishment of full-time officers and NCOs. The communists are quite accurate in using it in the sense of committed revolutionaries acting in groups as a nucleus around which the Party can grow, but it has become a cult word, invested with elite associations. Expensive schools have the same habit of coining a special word – 'toggers' or somesuch – for members of the first fifteen or others of the line-toeing elite.

CANUDING

verb. 'Nudespeak' for canoeing with nothing on.

'CANUDING is fine on quieter waterways ...' (An entry about the Yorkshire Sun Society, in *Inland Free Sun*, a NATURIST guidebook, 1988)

CAREER PATHS

noun. A maze of runways constituting the Rat Race.

'The structure of the group, with its three separate consultancies gives marketing direction and provides CAREER PATHS for senior EXECUTIVES.' (Copy in a brochure launching Shandwick plc on the unlisted securities market, 1985)

CARING

adjective. Meddlesome, intrusive, mischievous, snooping, trouble-making, officious, impertinent, prying.

CASH-FLOW ANALYSIS

compound noun. A neat philosophical CONSTRUCT which only sometimes bridges the gap between 'How much do we need?' and 'How much have we got?'

CEASE-FIRE

noun. A truce brought into line with modern thinking by the ease with which it can be unilaterally abrogated. Often it is a purely notional truce, existing only in the minds of statesmen and their press representatives, while the battle rages unabated. A CEASE-FIRE often has a 'line' (as in CEASE-FIRE line) – an imaginary boundary across which the antagonists continue to hurl staggering quantities of ammunition at each other.

CENSORSHIP

noun. The vindictive failure of publishers and broadcasters to give your views the prominence they deserve.

'These guardians of the cultural canon, practicing [*sic*] institutional repression and CENSORSHIP, have never presented sufficiently developed arguments for their exclusion of Haacke's work ...', (Benjamin Buchloch, writing in *ART in America*, February 1988)

The quotation refers to museum organisers and the like who decline to exhibit Mr Haacke's work. It is a significant extension of the use of the word CENSORSHIP. From meaning the *prohibition* (usually official) of publication, it now means the refusal to *assist* publication. (See HEGEMONIC).

CEREBRAL

adjective. A pejorative applied to the activities of the head by one who holds that the sensations of the heart take precedence.

Among those who positively enjoy the activities of their heads, CEREBRAL is a term of approval. Even works of modern ART, which display no vestige of having exercised the little grey cells, can earn the accolade CEREBRAL if the onlooker is sufficiently over-excited.

CHARISMA

noun. In theological terms, the God-given component of sainthood. That a word suggesting the essence of saintliness should be indiscriminately applied to such figures as President Kennedy and the frightful Yahoos of professional sport, shows how sadly it has come down in the world.

'As an act of total immersion ... the work is convincing and CHARISMATIC.' (Andrew Sinclair reviewing *Lenin: the Novel*, by Alan Brien, *The Times*, 22.10.87)

Here a book about history's leading atheist has aquired the God-given component of sainthood. Had Mr Sinclair been reviewing a lighter work in a more popular paper, he might perhaps have said 'convincing and spellbinding'. Otherwise it is difficult to see how Mr Brien's book can have CHARISMA even to the limited extent that Presidents and SPORTSMEN have it.

CHEESY-FOOTBALLS *adjective*. Describing the quality, I hope mistakenly, of Cossart's Bual Reserve Madeira. I have never played football, but I can imagine that after 80 minutes in close association with SPORTSMEN a football does indeed become cheesy. But is this a desirable characteristic in something that you are going to swallow? Apparently it is.

'Jane Hunt, a Master of Wine and a past winner of the annual scholarship offered by the Madeira wine institute, described this as having "a classic CHEESY-FOOTBALLS nose".' (*Wine*, New Year 1988)

Jane's nose, as opposed to the Madeira's nose, appears to be a most discriminating organ, but perhaps not suited to the wine trade. The analogies that suggest themselves to her as she samples the bouquet are not necessarily those that the manufacturer would choose to advertise his wares. Apropos of another Cossart product, their Duo Centenary Celebration Bual, she remarked that it smelt of 'plastic swimming pools'.

Stephen Potter's character, Odoreida, insisted that all wine comment should be entirely meaningless, like 'Too many tramlines'. 'Plastic swimming pools' is good, but not good enough.

CHIEF EXECUTIVE *noun*. The managing director of a company grown so large that there is no longer any hope of directing its management, or managing its direction.

CHILD *noun*. The catalyst which transforms the female condition of being 99% self-absorbed into being 101% self-absorbed.

CHILD ABUSE *noun.* The only circumstances in which KIDS are allowed the dignity of becoming children. CHILD ABUSE is the term used by the CARING and CONCERNED to cover a wide range of activities from rape and incest down to bullying in the playground. The most emotionally potent wedge which professional busybodies have attempted to hammer into the crumbling fabric of privacy and liberty.

'I am currently conducting research for Luton Rape Crisis Centre into the long term effects of CHILD sexual ABUSE on adult women ...' (Kathy French, letter to *Spare Rib*, January 1988)

Goodness. The baby rapes the nurse, and quite athwart goes all decorum. However, except to a frivolous mind it must be clear that MS French means the effect on women of ABUSE when they were children, and this is ABUSE used as a blanket term (if you will excuse the expression). For more precise ABUSE we must turn to the MARXISTS.

' ... few have ever been in the paediatrician's position, examining the swollen bottom and inflamed anus of a sexually-ABUSED child.' (Ann Spackman, writing in *MARXISM TODAY*, January 1988)

Anyone who has been to a good school knows what this is, but MS Spackman was obviously not a close student of the all-Great Britain 1987 Cleveland CHILD ABUSE saga. The whole point was that the paediatricians were not confronted by obvious symptoms of this lurid kind. The evidence of ABUSE was an untested and controversial diagnostic technique that involved prodding the child's bottom and observing its reaction. In similar circumstances in America (where they always find a word for these things) the counsel for the children's parents described the technique as 're-rape'.

Obviously to BUGGER or rape a child is a very serious matter, and the same term should not be used to lump such acts together with less important forms of molestation.

POLITICIANS, of course, are addicted to kissing babies, but this malpractice is usually hushed up for fear of scarring the child's psyche.

CHRISTIANITY

noun. The world's largest religion, with over one billion followers. It has achieved this enviable position of MARKET LEADERSHIP by the time-honoured business technique of diversification. CHRIST-IANITY has subdivided into more sects and denominations than any of the other great religions, but all share the central proposition that Jesus Christ was the son of God.

It is not, however, the divinity of Christ that is the real attraction of CHRISTIANITY. The reason for CHRIST-IANITY's popularity is a brilliant psychological *coup de main – it enables people to feel virtuous about their faults.* Breast-beating is its characteristic posture. Like many other products of mankind's imagination, it obeys the Law of Opposites. The virtues recommended by its founder are the very last qualities you expect to find in the conduct of the CHRISTIAN churches – just as music is the last thing you expect to hear on the Music Programme, and Added Value is the last thing you expect to get from VALUE ADDED TAX.

There are five main subdivisions of CHRISTIANITY: the Orthodox, or mystical, obedience; the Catholic, or pragmatic, obedience; the Protestant, or general utility, obedience; the Coptic, or forgotten, obedience; and the Church of England.

Which obedience you choose is a matter of taste. The Orthodox Church offers the finest music and ceremonial. The Catholic Church appears to be the most sympathetic to the wrongdoer – until you read the small print of the contract. The Protestant Churches are the most easily reconciled with intellectual honesty. The Coptic Church was once rife among the Egyptians, but has been supplanted by ISLAM and bilharzia. The Church of England was a praiseworthy attempt to introduce constitutional government, the rule of law, and all the other blessings of British Administration to the Kingdom of Heaven, but unfortunately God proved quite as recalcitrant as the Americans, the Irish, the Boers, the Zulus, and countless other aborigines, and Heavens remains a theocratic state.

CINEMA VERITÉ   *noun.* Cinema at even its least truthful. The fraudulent technique of simulating documentary film in what is actually a carefully rehearsed and staged drama. Subsequenly given the marginally-more-honest name of 'Faction', CINEMA VERITÉ falls into the sacred category of realism, and is, revealingly, the favourite cinematic mode both of those who deal in COMPASSION, and of those who deal in violence.

CIVIL DEFENCE

noun. A number of expedients designed to mitigate the effects of nuclear attack. CIVIL DEFENCE is very popular in the USSR and Switzerland, but lags behind in Britain where it is feared that the mere suggestion of such measures might provoke the USSR into immediate and unrestrained thermo-nuclear war.

CIVIL SERVANTS

noun. Our insolent masters.

Masters also of circumlocution. In 1948 Sir Ernest Gowers was invited by the Treasury to write a book 'to help officials in their use of written English as a tool of their trade'.

The result was *Plain Words*, a scholarly, well-mannered and humorous attack on official jargon.

Alas, British CIVIL SERVANTS attach more importance to being earnest than to heeding Ernest, and they continue to speak and write slovenly, illiterate and misleading English as if their lives depended on it.

Which of course they do. There is no need for me to provide an example. Seek out your last VALUE ADDED TAX form, or find a friend who is VAT registered, and pore over its incomprehensible phrases. While you pore, reflect on the penalties you or your friend will suffer if you fail to understand and obey them.

That is why Gowers went unheeded. CIVIL SERVANTS need nonsense to lay a snare for you, so that they may exercise their over-mighty powers and slake their thirst for tyranny.

CLIENT BASE

noun. What a businessman calls his customers. There are two reasons for this piece of pomposity The first is that in businesses – like banking – where there is no PRODUCT, some suggesion of concrete structure – 'BASE' – greatly eases the mind of the businessman who feels himself to be floundering in a sea of abstraction. It might even be possible that there is no substance to his business whatsoever, and that it requires only the pricking of the bubble, the collapse of the market, to send him spinning into bankruptcy. A CLIENT BASE, therefore, is a comforting suggestion of solidity and permanence.

The second reason is less creditable. Professionals, like lawyers, have CLIENTS. Tradesmen have customers. Bankers, stockbrokers, and others involved in the manipulation of money, are unquestionably tradesmen. They even use the word 'trading' to describe some of their activities. But the huge sums that stick to their fingers have willy-nilly propelled them into higher strata of society, and they feel the need to dignify their calling.

'NIKKO's extensive CLIENT BASE ... '
(NIKKO Securities Annual Report, 1986).

What is meant is 'NIKKO's many Japanese customers.'

Social workers have this, if nothing else, in common with businessmen. They too call their victims 'CLIENTS'.

COLLATERAL DAMAGE   *noun.* A consequence of the way in which civilians *will* gatecrash battles, without even the pretence of having been invited.

COLLECTIVE   *adjective.* Used of the will, activities and property of the group, as dictated by the group's party-appointed leader.

COMBAT EMPLACEMENT EVACUATOR   *noun.* The bluff, military way of calling a spade a spade.

COMMITMENT
noun. What the modern zealot calls his zealotry – or, more often, hers.

COMMUNICATOR
noun. He who can, does. He who cannot, teaches. He who can't even teach, COMMUNICATES.

COMPREHENSIVE EDUCATION
*noun.*1. An attempt by egalitarians to iron out inequalities of intellect in the young by refusing to teach any of them anything.

2. A system for producing the raw materials of SOCIALISM – young, incompetent, dependent, ill-instructed, illiterate, electoral cannon fodder.

(See also EDUCATION, PAINTERLY VALUES, and DESKILLING.)

COMPUTER LITERATE
adjective. Being able to associate the pressing of certain keys (INPUT) with certain consequences (OUTPUT). Animals are perfectly able to perform feats of this kind, but will not do so unless they are sure that food will result. Creatures lower on the scale of intelligence than animals will mindlessly tap away, in a vacuous trance, without any hope of reward.

'You must be COMPUTER LITERATE and have well-developed marketing skills together with good all-round public relations experience.' (Job advertisement placed by Applied Management Services in *The Times*, 18.11.87)

Very soon human beings will not have to undertake these soul-destroying forms of drudgery. If BEHAVIOURAL ENRICH-MENT lives up to expectations, every agency in the land will soon be full of orang-utans gleefully tapping the keyboards.

CONCERN

noun. An interest in other people's affairs.

CONCEPT

noun. An idea entertained by one who feels unsure of the value of ideas, and therefore likes to associate them with earthy notions of insemination and procreation.

> 'A CONCEPT is an object in the world of the mind.' (Edward de Bono, *Wordpower*, 1977)

In one sense no-one could accuse Dr de Bono of being unsure of the value of ideas. He thrives on them. The value of his ideas, expressed in royalties, must be considerable. Perhaps it is the contemplation of their value which causes him to wander a bit when discussing them.

> 'The CONCEPT includes not only an acknowledgement of the physical object but also of its use and perhaps a parcel of associations that are usually attached to it.' (*Ibid.*)

Even if you place the words 'not only' where they belong, you are still left with 'a parcel of associations' floating indecisively about. Are they being included, or acknowledged, or is acknowledgement of them included?

If he means what I think he means, the sentence should read: 'The CONCEPT includes the recognition not only of the physical object, but also of its use, and perhaps of a parcel of associations that are usually attached to it.' For a man who has written (among many others) 11 books whose titles include the words 'mind' or 'thinking', the quoted sentence is dramatically ill-organised.

> 'I invented the term "LATERAL THINKING" to describe the CONCEPT that involved changes in CONCEPTS or

approaches to a problem.' (*Ibid.*) (See also LATERAL THINKING.)

One does see that the term LATERAL THINKING was very necessary to Dr de Bono, whose CONCEPTS change like quicksilver under the impact of his 'thinking techniques'.

They remain ideas for all that.

CONFIDENTIALITY   *noun.* An obligation not to disclose the TRUTH. Doctors have a rule to treat their patients' revelations in confidence. This is an obvious professional necessity. Few patients would return if they thought that their urticaria was the subject of merriment at the doctor's dinner table. But the more unctuous doctors become about CONFIDENTIALITY, the more you can be sure that something is afoot.

CONFIDENTIALITY is paraded most often to defend the practice of prescribing contraceptives to under-age girls. The doctor's judgement about the effects of pregnancy on the girl's health is held to take precedence over all other considerations, and CONFIDENTIALITY is the excuse for not informing her legal guardians. Having carnal knowledge of a minor is a crime, and I do not see how doctors can escape the inference that they are aiding and abetting crime, even though the crime is committed not by the patient, but by the party of the second part. And, other than puffing themselves up with professional gravitas, how do doctors justify a mere professional obligation taking precedence over the legal RIGHTS of the child's parents or guardians?

The other great CONFIDENTIALITY

tricksters are journalists. 'Never disclose your sources' is their proud motto. The more exhibitionist sort of journalist has actually gone to jail rather than reveal his sources. And rightly. There is no reason why a piece of professional etiquette should overrule the legal obligation to tell the whole truth in the witness box.

In fairness to journalists, it must be added that the plea of CONFIDENTI-ALITY is often a desperate last resort. Their story having been entirely fabricated in the first place, there is no source to betray. But it would never do to say so.

CONFRONTATION *noun.* The art of waging war, or conducting any lesser dispute, without actually coming to grips.

CONSCIOUSNESS *noun.* A condition, invariably heightened, in which the modern elect exist. A state of intellectual and spiritual alertness. For those who normally feel about as alert as a stunned mullet, there are 'consciousness-raising therapies'.

> 'The typical CONSCIOUSNESS-raising group is composed of six to twelve women who meet on an average once a week.' (Unattributed entry in the anthology *Radical Feminism*, Quadrangle Books, New York, 1973)

So far, so good.

> 'Groups larger than ten or twelve are less conducive to lengthy personal discussion and analysis.' (*Ibid.*)

O dear.

> 'Generally CONSCIOUSNESS-raising groups spend from three to six months talking about personal experiences and

then analysing those experiences in feminist terms'. (*Ibid.*)

The mullet is a handsome fish, and there is much to be said for being stunned. When they are thoroughly analysed, these women go on to organise 'speak-outs' about rape, motherhood and abortion. The checklist of questions for this CONSCIOUSNESS-raising group covers exactly the same ground as any other hen-party, but rendered ponderous by the earnestness of the Feminists: Parents, puberty, men, marriage, men, motherhood, men, orgasm, beauty, men, ageing, and men.

CONSERVATIONIST

noun and *adjective*. 'One who conserves', or 'descriptive of conserving'. The correct derivation from the verb 'to conserve' should, of course, be CONSERVATIVE ...
You see the difficulty.

CONSERVATISM

noun. A political philosophy – peculiar to Great Britain – which holds change to be synonymous with decay.

CONSORTIUM

noun. A troupe of performing profiteers, held together, like acrobats, by the knowledge that the first man to fall takes the rest with him.

CONSTRUCT

noun. An association of words or ideas too loose to be called an argument. A borrowing from mathematics, with agreeable echoes of 'structure' and its associated workmanship.

'Television is, like nations [*sic*], a CONSTRUCT of specific institutions; what it "means" turns on how these institutional DISCOURSES CON-STRUCT it for their own specific purposes.' (John Hartley, 'Invisible Fiction, television audiences, PAEDOCRACY, pleasure', an article in the magazine *Textual Practice*, Summer 1987)

If this rigmarole means anything it is: 'Television is controlled by institutions.'

Mr Hartley displays a well-developed conspiracy mania. The institutions, you notice, are left unnamed, and their wicked deliberations are wrapped up in abstractions like DISCOURSES and CONSTRUCTS.

Of course television is controlled by institutions – in as far as anything controls such a huge apparatus. The alternatives are control by an individual or by the state. (See also PAEDOCRACY.)

CONSTRUCTION INDUSTRY

noun. Hi-tech builders. A blithe conspiracy to make the creations of modern ARCHITECTS fall down as quickly as possible. A very free masonry.

CONSUMER

noun. The commercial equivalent of the Strasbourg Goose, the CONSUMER replaces the customer, to whom the supplier had inconvenient obligations.

'Customer' also found little favour among ECONOMISTS. Customers come and go. They assert themselves, and exercise choice. They refuse to fit into categories and patterns, and thereby seriously disrupt the purity of economic theory. They had to go, and they had to be replaced by an indistinguishable, undiscriminating mob, like pigs round a trough – the CONSUMERS.

CONTEMPORARY

adjective. Hideous, dull, and incomprehensible, as in 'CONTEMPORARY dance'.

'Yet, on another level, the film engages the viewer in a complex relationship with issues confronting CONTEMPORARY culture.' (Coco Fusco, writing in *ART in America*, February 1988)

It had to be 'on another level', didn't it? As for the rest of it, why not: 'The film makes the viewer think about modern culture.'? It would be difficult for a film to 'engage' a viewer in a 'relationship' even with one of the characters in the film, never mind with an outside abstraction like 'issues confronting CONTEMPORARY culture'.

Reviewers use CONTEMPORARY to mean up-to-date, or modern. The shrewd reader will spot immediately that this is not what it means. It means 'belonging to the same time', or, if I really want to make myself understood where it will count, 'Accessing the same timeframe'.

CONTROLLED EXPLOSION

noun. An explosion from whose vicinity all human beings have been removed, and most military personnel.

CORE CURRICULUM

noun. The irreducible components of literacy and numeracy which teachers cannot avoid imparting, whatever their objections.

CORPORATE ENTERTAINMENT

noun. Booze-ups for businessmen.

'*Alliance*, though designed using the latest techniques retains a traditional air that befits a yacht whose primary role is CORPORATE ENTERTAINMENT ...' (Comment on a mega-million dollar yacht in *Boat International*, January 1988)

There is much to be said for CORPORATE ENTERTAINMENT afloat. Any yacht, mega-million or otherwise, can be sent to the bottom with all hands.

CORPORATE IDENTITY

noun. What business organisations have instead of military uniforms, badges, insignia, mottoes, mascots, buttons, colours and shiny boots. A collection of morale-ENHANCING devices employed to persuade the HUMAN RESOURCES of modern commerce that they in some way share the glory of their employer's wealth. A sizeable chunk of that wealth is shared, not by the employees, but by the wily denizens of the design community who charge FABULOUS fees for CREATING that elusive thing – a CORPORATE IDENTITY.

Nor is the money entirely wasted, since a CORPORATE IDENTITY frequently serves as a smokescreen between a company and the public, veiling the true nature of its activities. For instance a company that manufactures noxious materials might choose a rare and fragrant bird as its emblem. Or an organisation manufacturing lethal weapons might choose some such motto as 'Peace in Security'.

CORPORATION

noun. An old-fashioned euphemism for 'belly' or 'gut'. Nowadays it refers not to human disfigurement, but to a firm or company with adiposity problems. Abnormally and disgustingly fat companies become 'multinational CORPOR-ATIONS'. As with human beings,

beings, business adiposity can be the result of an unfortunate glandular condition – or just plain overeating. Or both. The first of these two conditions is serious and irreversible. It occurs when the mechanism that controls the number of EXECUTIVES in the company bloodstream breaks down, and these parasitic cells multiply uncontrollably, obliterating the red cell count in the CORPORATION's CASH FLOW. Eliminating the EXECUTIVES is of no avail, since dozens spring up for each one got rid of. It is sometimes called Parkinson's (Law) Disease.

COUNSELLING *noun.* The outward manifestation of COMPASSION. The mode of procedure of social workers, clergymen, some doctors, and all busybodies. The tendering of unwanted advice.

'Centre for Advancement of Counselling Certificate in COUNSELLING ... Students may be new to COUN-SELLING, exploring an interest, or currently COUNSELLING. Applicants are welcomed from the voluntary and statutory sectors of social services, and HEALTH, EDUCATION, industry, commerce, government and police There are two courses, one based on theory and the other skills. Students completing both courses will be eligible for the ADVANCED CERTIFICATE IN COUNSELLING.' (Advertisement in the *Guardian*, 6.1.88)

And they shall be called Wonderful, Counsellors ...

'Adlerian WORKSHOPS and publications is [*sic*] offering the following courses and seminars during the next year:

Crisis COUNSELLING
Grief and bereavement
Impasse Priority Therapy
Living beyond Grief
Problems and Problem Solving
Towards a DEMOCRATIC approach
   to discipline
Adlerian WORKSHOPS and publications, formed in 1985, offers an ONGOING series of seminars, WORKSHOPS and intensive courses on a wide variety of topics, particularly appropriate and relevant to those working in the social, welfare and medical professions.' (Advertisement in *New Society*, 22.1.88)

Those who go about doing deliberate good bear a sufficiently heavy burden of responsibility already without adding offences against the language to the charge sheet. 'Impasse Priority Therapy' means, I suppose, 'curing indecision'. There is something almost indelicate in this preoccupation with the grief of others. If you were in a crisis or impasse; if you had been bereaved, or were intent on living beyond grief; if you had a problem with your DEMOCRATIC approach to discipline – would you welcome the attentions of an Adlerian graduate?

COUNTER INTUITIVE   *adjective.* Having the intuition that not all is well with intuition.

COUNTERPARTY   *noun.* The partner-in-crime of a counter-jumper.

CREATIVE   *adjective.* Slavishly adherent to the views of one's employer – as in CREATIVE writer, CREATIVE designer etc., seen in job advertisements.

'Senior CREATIVE writer ... a CON-CEPTUAL writer with at least 5 years' experience is sought by this energetic and expanding Surrey-based agency ... Candidates must demonstrate CREATIVE skills and the capacity to INTERFACE well both with clients and art directors.' (Advertisement by Mitchell Marketing and Communications Ltd in *The Times*, 27.1.88)

I think 'INTERFACING well' counts as slavish adherence.

CREDIBILITY

noun. The quality said to be possessed by one who is obviously lying, but whose views correspond with those of the listener. CREDIBILITY is not the same as 'plausibility', as it operates on an altogether higher and more abstract plane. People who have CREDIBILITY often have CHARISMA.

CREDIT CONTROLLER

noun. A dun or debt collector. An officer employed by any large organisation to write you letters of baleful purport whenever your bills are overdue.

CROSS-CULTURAL COMMUNICATION

noun. Interchanges that are frequently cross but never cultural.

CUBE

noun. According to the *OED*, a CUBE is a solid figure contained by six equal squares. This doesn't seem to admit of much variation, but modern ARCHITECTS and their admirers are not daunted by difficulties of this restricting kind.

'Chicago is a great city, and it has many CUBE-like buildings. A lot of buildings on the great palazzos [*sic*] of Florence are CUBES. Classical buildings are often

CUBES.' (Jane Robins, talking to Richard Rogers, designer of the Centre Pompidou, Paris, and the Lloyd's Building, London, in *Square Mile*, 1984)

I will concede that Chicago has many CUBE-*like* buildings, which may account for its being so criminous and uninhabitable. The great palaces of Florence do not have cubic buildings on them, nor are they themselves CUBES, even when they stand on a Piazza. I think that disposes of most of Miss Robins's misapprehensions about Florence.

I will give Miss Robins a toffee for every classical building she can show me that is a solid figure contained on six sides by equal squares.

These words (which do not make clear whether Mr Rogers is being quoted indirectly, or whether they are Miss Robins's own interpolations) were written in praise of the proposed Mies van der Rohe building for Mansion House Square. It is precisely because of this compulsive thinking in terms of abstractions – voids, space, CUBES, volumes – that modern buildings are so banal, brutal, hideous, unoriginal and uninhabitable. (See ENRICH.)

CULTURAL AGGRESSION *noun*. Offending other people's sensibilities in a way that cannot be classified as racial or political.

"Foreign tourists found bathing in the nude at the Indian resort of Goa should be deported to prevent CULTURAL AGGRESSION", a member of the ruling Congress party told India's parliament yesterday.' (A report in the *Daily Telegraph*, 29.3.88)

The unnamed member of parliament displays a perfectly-proportioned persecution mania. There he stands, at the head of the largest democracy on earth, and is capable of feeling CULTURALLY put-upon by a few foreign NATURISTS. It is true that the naked form is profoundly shocking both to Muslims and Hindus, and both communities are sunk in the most abject BODY GUILT and 'clothes compulsion' – to borrow two items of Nudespeak. Shocking enough, perhaps, for the tourists' activities to seem in the fevered mind of a zealot to be an aggressive attempt to foist their standards on the local community.

Goa fosters a large Catholic population, courtesy of years of Portuguese rule, which is also rather down on the bared boob. Since the NATURISTS have succeeded (where for 200 years the British failed) in finding a unifying cause for India's divided society, might they not be allowed to stay?

On the other hand, perhaps the Congressman has it in mind to open a Bikini Boutique in Goa.

CULTURAL REVOLUTION

noun. A violent and barbaric attempt to preserve a threatened status quo, in which the few vestiges of culture remaining in Mao's China were heavily sat upon.

CULTUREBUS

noun. A sealed, sterilised capsule in which tourists are preserved from the bacilli of civilisation.

D

DAMAGE LIMITATION

noun. The exhilarating sport of trying to shoot the cat after it has been let out of the bag.

Originating in the dangerous world of naval warfare – DAMAGE LIMITATION parties got to work as soon as a vessel was hit – the term now designates the equally frantic efforts of politicians and their henchmen to smother the flames of TRUTH on the rare occasions they are allowed to break out.

DATA BASE

noun. The records of any organisation unwise enough to employ computers. A trackless swamp into which all useful information disappears, and from which it cannot be retrieved in recognisable shape.

'*Beyond the Spreadsheet.* We can expect multidimensional models defined in English to take snapshots of data from the CORPORATE DATA BASE for processing on a PC.' (Headline and introduction from an article in *Accountancy*, November 1987)

Silly us! We had forgotten multidimensional models. They will rescue us from the trackless swamp, and do it 'defined in English' – an assurance that would be comforting were it not incredible. The versatile little chaps are going to take photographs too.

The headline sounds like one of the degrees of bastardy.

DEADLY EMBRACE   *noun.* Computerists love to dignify the dull mathematics of their trade with exciting, even sensational, terminology. A DEADLY EMBRACE is the mutual posture of two computers whose programmers have instructed each that it cannot proceed without consulting the other. There is no protocol to overcome this impasse, and the two machines squat there, glaring and baffled, like two members of a golf club who have not been introduced, unable to go further.

DECISION-MAKING PROCESS   *noun.* A sequence of observances ritually followed by the senior hierophants of the bureaucracy. A shuttle system criss-crossing Whitehall that keeps the sacred files and memos in perpetual circulation.

DEDICATION   *noun.* Similar to COMMITMENT but more widespread. Almost every organisation boasts that its staff is DEDICATED. Even WORD PROCESSORS can be DEDICATED – an obscure usage which seems to indicate simple WORD PROCESSORS which lack – primitive machines – any DATA BASE.

DELEGATE   *verb.* To practise the art of simultaneously bullying and blaming your subordinates.

DEMOCRACY   *noun.* An adaptable word that completely reverses its meaning when preceded by the word 'People's'.

Since *demos* is already incorporated in DEMOCRACY, this is no doubt an example of two positives making a negative.

DEREGULATION   *noun.* Forgetting the lessons of 1929 and reverting to the extravagant practices of

1928, with predictable results. (See BIG BANG.)

DESIGNER   *noun.* One employed to hide defective workmanship behind matching accessories, and worthless writing behind exotic typefaces. (See ARTWORK and CORPORATE IDENTITY).

DESIGNER CLOTHES   *noun.* Clothes cut to suggest that the wearer has designs on you, or wishes to stimulate designs in you.

DESKILLING   *noun.* The moderns are in a quandary about 'skills'. In all menial and repetitive activities skills are greatly to be desired. There are even 'Skills Centres' where the unemployed can intensify their unemployability. Even those as high up the social scale as social workers boast of their 'skills'. Managers have skills. And so on.

But in the ARTS they will never do. Skills are the dross of an outworn tradition. Away with them! (See PAINTERLY VALUES.)

But here is one who – though unmistakably a modern – seems to be having doubts:

'While arguments can be made in favour of discarding "anachronistic" practices in the face of "space age" technologies, what is so often overlooked is that skills are not merely manual dexterity but forms of knowledge. The acquisition of particular skills implies an access to a body of accumulated knowledge. Thus DESKILLING means a rupture with an historical body of knowledge – in other words, a dehistoricization of the practice of ART.' (Ian Burn, 'The Sixties: Crisis and Aftermath' *Art and Text*, Vol. 1, Autumn 1981)

Did he have to find 'other words'? He was doing fairly well up to that point, though DESKILLING is frightful. You would have thought he could fall no further, even in other words. But he succeeds effortlessly. 'Dehistoricization' is worse than frightful. It's utterly DE-SKILLED.

DESKILLING, therefore, is the process touched on under COMPREHENSIVE EDUCATION and PAINTERLY VALUES – the process of not teaching pupils anything, usually in case they should outshine the teacher.

The term was originally used to describe the process (which left-wing sociologists claimed to detect in capitalist societies) of deliberately eliminating manual skills to enslave the working classes to the capitalists' machines. The early capitalists were not as well organised as that, but modern educationalists and ART pundits are.

DETAINEE *noun*. The coy recipient of the importunate hospitality of the state. A prisoner who has not had the decency to legitimise his arrest by committing an offence. A speck of grit in the gleaming machinery of state. A corpus with a surfeit of habeas.

DETENTE *noun*. An *entente incordiale*. The reconciliation of two irreconcilable parties. The drawing together of two antagonists always likely to spring apart, like a man trying to tie together the ends of two very powerful bits of elastic.

'East-West DETENTE' is the most frequent example, but there is no reason to

rule out 'Arab-Israeli DETENTE', 'Cath-
olic-Protestant DETENTE', and many
more.

DEVELOPING — *adjective*. Passing from the twilight of
empire into the Stygian night of one-party
rule. (See LDCs).

DEVOLUTION — *noun*. Allowing the Scots and Welsh and –
above all – the Northern Irish to go their
own ways now that their usefulness has
been expended.

DIALECTIC — *noun*. A mode of enquiry bearing the same
relation to reason as belief in ghosts to
religion. A system of debased philosophies
of convenience enabling the user to
categorise his opponent as morally,
socially, or politically undesirable, without
reference to the validity of his arguments.

> 'Every DIALECTICAL philosophy of
> the relations of knowledge and experi-
> ences provides the subject matter for a
> bureaucracy of the spirit, which presents
> itself as the organ, both visible and
> mysterious, in whose name this DIA-
> LECTIC operates.' (Jean-François Lyo-
> tard, *Dérive à Partir de Marx et Freud*,
> Paris, 1973)

I do not fully understand this reference,
but it seems to me that M. Lyotard and I
share a low opinion of DIALECTICS. I do
not, however, share the only 'thought' that
I can discern behind this sentence, which is
an old one, and certainly needs new words
if M. Lyotard is not to be suspected of
INTERTEXTUALITY with the Romantic
poets.
　What I think he is saying is: organised
knowledge makes a prison for the spirit,

and becomes its own end, instead of a means to an end.

The tyranny of intellectual discipline has long been bewailed. The dull brain, after all, perplexes and retards The point that M. Lyotard misses is that it is only the *dull* brain which has this effect. If you unleash Messieurs Marx, Freud and Lyotard on a problem, you will indeed become perplexed and retarded. Other intellects have a more enlightening effect.

Keats must be updated: Though the DIALECTIC brain perplexes and retards.

DIALOGUE

noun. A cacophony of simultaneous monologues.

'*From the Archbishop of York.* Sir, I feel impelled to comment on your leading article's (November 16th) singularly ungenerous reference to myself. To accuse me of ungenerously wanting only "DIALOGUE with Christians" in the Conservative Party when I was in process of defending a report which advocates the widest possible discussion in such matters across religious and cultural barriers seems perverse to say the least.

My reference to "DIALOGUE with Christians" was directed towards what was already happening. If the Conservative Party as such wants constructive conversations about its philosophy with the Church of England, no one would welcome it more than I. Yours faithfully, John Ebor, etc. (Letter to *The Times*, 10.11.87)

No stylist, Ebor. The repeated 'ungenerous'; the misplaced 'only'; 'as such'; and 'constructive', all tell against him. But one gets his drift.

Are there any Christians in the Conservative Party? Such a suggestion is surely actionable? I suspect that Ebor, in his heart of hearts, would agree that no DIALOGUE between the Church and the Conservative Party in their present guises could be anything other than a cacophony of simultaneous monologues.

DIFFERENTIAL

noun. 1. The bit inserted into the transmission of a motor car to baffle the amateur mechanic and ensure employment for the professional.

2. By extension of the first meaning, the margin by which the pay of a trade unionist must exceed that of the amateurs who do not belong to his union.

DIRECT DEMOCRACY

noun. An interesting variant on People's DEMOCRACY concocted by Colonel Qaddafi of Libya, in which the Leader of the Revolution gives directions to the masses, which they enthusiastically and democratically endorse.

DIRECT MASS DEMOCRACY

noun. Mob rule. Threatening behaviour. Making demands with menaces. Causing an affray. Tactics which, when used by right-wing political groups, provoke well-merited charges of FASCISM. When used by the left, it is better to leave them to incriminate themselves, which they do effortlessly.

' ... we were deliberately following a policy of substituting DIRECT MASS DEMOCRACY for any form of decision making structure. The meetings were clumsy, brilliant, interminable and exhilarating; it would be quite wrong to pretend that we students at least were motivated by anything other than fla-grant contempt for BOURGEOIS Liberal niceties.' (Jem Thomas, describ-ing himself as a 'former Essex student', letter to the *Guardian*, 9.5.88)

I don't think 'flagrant' is the word Mr Thomas needs. Can even his contempt be 'flaming' or 'afire'? Can it be 'openly scandalous'? But I imagine he was too taken up with DIRECT MASS DEMO-CRACY to bother about dull things like English – if indeed such refinements of scholarship were available at Essex in 1968. For it is to the exciting events of that year that Mr Thomas's letter refers.

He describes with glee what fun they all had breaking up other people's meetings, and holding their own clumsy and intermi-nable ones, which he nonetheless found 'exhilarating' and 'brilliant'.

It is sad to reflect that these were Mr Thomas's salad days, and that he has probably not had so much fun since. (See DEMOCRACY.)

DIRECT-RESPONSE *adjective.* Used of a method of selling by telephone which often elicits a response more direct than the salesman desires.

DISADVANTAGED *adjective.* A description of the sort of poverty experienced by the 'clients' of a Social Worker. The adjective 'poor' is thought to have ELITIST overtones, and has the additional drawback of being accurate.

DISAMBIGUATE *verb.* For once the definition is provided – whole and pure – by the nonsenseer himself.

'Similarly we can DISAMBIGUATE (resolve the ambiguity of) *Egyptian cotton shirt* by having the first cut after *Egyptian* (a cotton shirt made in Egypt) or after *cotton* (a shirt made of Egyptian cotton) ...' (Frank Palmer, *Grammar*, Penguin Books, 1971)

In the interests of thoroughly ambiguating the whole topic, what about a shirt made of Egyptian cotton in Egypt?

DISC JOCKEY

*noun.*1. The only organism produced by evolution that has developed the power of speech without first evolving a mind.
2. The modern equivalent of the court jester. But while the court jester could look his monarch in the face to decide how his jokes were going down, the DISC JOCKEY has no contact with his public. *Demos* kills coldly, and from a distance. The DISC JOCKEY must talk, talk, talk, desperately, mindlessly and continuously, to prevent his listeners from switching off.

DISCOURSE

noun (from French *discours*, and German *diskurs*). A term used by STRUCTU-RALISTS and POST-STRUCTURALISTS to mean the underlying theoretical discussion which, they insist, must be at the bottom of every social phenomenon, concrete or abstract. There is of course no need for these interchanges to be described or recognised. They are there, part of the 'structure' or basis of thought. Here is a POST-STRUCTURALIST in his 'DIS-COURSE mode', analysing freely.

'That is the traditional question. The one I would prefer to pose is rather different. Compared to the traditional, noble and philosophic question it is much more down to earth and concrete. My problem is rather this: what rules of right are implemented by the relations of power in the production of DISCOUR-SES of TRUTH? Or, alternatively, what type of power is susceptible of producing DISCOURSES of TRUTH that in a society such as ours are endowed with such potent effects? What I mean is this: in a society such as ours, but basically in any society, there are manifold relations of power which permeate, characterize and constitute the social body, and these relations of power cannot themselves be established, consolidated nor implemented without the production, accumulation, circulation and functioning of a DISCOURSE. There can be no possible exercise of *power* without a certain economy of DISCOURSES of truth which operates through and on the basis of this association.' (Michel Foucault, *Power/Knowledge: Selected Interviews and Other Writings 1972-1977*, Pantheon Books, 1977)

There are two possible explanations of this kind of writing. The first and more probable is that Monsieur Foucault is not discussing anything at all. He is just spinning words – as grand and abstract as possible – in the all-too-likely hope of establishing an academic reputation, gaining disciples, and generally joining the modern elect. The second possibility is that he is too busy patronising traditional modes of describing things to understand that to express himself clearly a writer needs discipline and a modicum of humility.

DISCOURSE MODES   *noun.* Ways of speaking, talking or conversing.

'*The Linguistic Characteristics of DIS-COURSE MODES.* To this end I will outline the characteristics of five modes which I found in the talk of 10 to 12 year olds, referring to each mode in turn by the categorical label I have assigned to it.' (Terry Phillips, 'Beyond Lip Service: Discourse Development after the Age of Nine', an entry in *Language and Learning: an Interactional PERSPEC-TIVE*, the Falmer Press, 1985)

Nothing if not deliberate, our Terry. One might even say ponderous. And one might say it even more after reading the sequel to this introduction. These are the names (sorry, categorical labels) assigned by Terry to each of the five modes:

Hypothetical
Experiential
Argumentational
Operational
Expositional

Beneath this flurry of syllables Terry is telling us that he found ten to twelve year old children to be:

Given to asking questions
Given to relating their experiences
Argumentative
Bossy
Endlessly and incoherently explanatory

His biographical note reveals Terry to be a lecturer in the School of Education at the University of East Anglia. In this bleak and horrible spot he makes use 'of the relatively unfamiliar concept of discourse analysis' to show how 'the different discourse styles associated with each of these modes have profound implications for thinking and learning'. Terry himself has thought and learnt to the extent that he is able to express in his repellent jargon truths about ten year olds which any mother, be she never so distant from the ivory towers of

East Anglia, could have told him in pithy Anglo-Saxon.

DISINFORMATION   *noun.* A special category of government information actually acknowledged – albeit privily – to be misleading. (See MANAGED NEWS.)

DISINVITE   *verb.* To repudiate, renounce, rebuff, or discard. What you do to the guest whom you discover to be unwanted just before the event occurs. The academic equivalent of getting the footman to turn visitors away from the doorstep.

> 'With some reluctance the general purposes committee has therefore decided to take the line that would cause the least harm, i.e. to DISINVITE Nolte.' (Sir Raymond Hoffenberg, President of Wolfson College, Oxford, speaking of his college's decision to withdraw an invitation to Professor Ernst Nolte of the Free University of Berlin to participate in a series of lectures. Reported in the *Independent*, 24.10.88. See PRESTIGIOUS)

Professor Nolte's crime was to have suggested that the Germans were not alone in having slaughtered millions of people, with the implication that the ENORMITY of the Germans' offence was no worse for the fact that most of their victims were Jewish.

If you disregard race, and crudely add up the scores, the record bag belongs to the Communist bloc, and is so huge that it seems unlikely ever to be beaten. Besides, Professor Nolte's point is a very obvious one. There you are, formed up in front of the mass grave, with a flinty-faced executioner making his way along the line, plying his pistol. The general feeling of gloom must be the same regardless of whether you are there as a Jew, a Polish officer, a bourgeois reactionary, a Kulak, or someone inadequately appreciative of Chairman Mao.

But if you are naughty enough to approach the glamorous and seductive subject of slaughter dispassionately, DISINVITATION is the very least you can expect.

I don't recollect a Wolfson College, but a recent visit to Oxford suggests that it is a cylindrical building masquerading as a car park somewhere at the back of St Ebbes.

DISK

noun. The figment of a fevered imagination – like a flying saucer. A fabled, round, shining plate, rumoured to contain all knowledge and wisdom. The totem of a deluded cult of machine-worshippers.

DISTRIBUTIONAL COMPULSION

noun. The urge to buy off the lower orders by distributing existing wealth, rather than by making more wealth. A strong tendency that overcomes democratic societies with an aversion to work.

Affluence, runs the argument against DISTRIBUTIONAL COMPULSION, by satisfying needs that *can* be satisfied, sharpens appetites that cannot be satisfied (see POSITIONAL GOODS), and therefore breeds discontent. The more you satisfy material needs, the greater the clamour for unattainable desires will become.

'Hence the paradox of affluence. It embodies a DISTRIBUTIONAL COMPULSION, which in turn leads to our reluctant collectivism.' (Professor Fred Hirsch, *Social Limits to Growth*, Routledge and Kegan Paul, London, 1977)

To yield to your DISTRIBUTIONAL COMPULSION is very naughty. It destroys the 'distributional neutrality' of the competitive market. It deliberately distorts free market forces. Right-wing economists regard the market with devotional awe, and treat it with the pussyfooting respect accorded by the Pharisees to the sabbath. Left-wing economists, on the other hand, take the frivolous view that the market was made for man, not man for the market.

But the market, DISTRIBUTIONAL COMPULSION, and even the great economy itself, are all either generalisations or abstractions, and should be consigned to the great wagger of the mind.

DOG *noun.* A twelve-yearly reminder of mortality.

DOUBLE-VOLUME *adjective.* Describing the quality of a room without a ceiling, and therefore enjoying a prospect of the beams, rafters and other roof components traditionally hidden from view.

'Superb 3-bedroom house. DOUBLE-VOLUME recep. with open-plan gallery. Integral garage.' (An advertisement in the Parkway, N1 branch of Stickley and Kent, estate agents, October 1988)

It indicates a building so crude in its construction that not only is the roof exposed, but there is even a left-over bit where the bedrooms don't fit. You can drive the car into the hall as well.

DOUBTING THOMAS *noun.* One so mannerless as to question self-evidently absurd propositions. An insensitive lout who, if not firmly snubbed, might pull down the cosy edifice of belief and leave us shivering in the cold winds of truth. A tastless quibbler, demanding proof where no proof can be.

DYSFUNCTIONAL

adjective. The Greek-derived prefix 'dys' enjoys a widespread vogue among the nonsenseers, who love to tack it on to words of other-than-Greek origin, just to give us all some fun.

'Functional' and 'DYSFUNCTIONAL' are used by the medics to mean 'affecting the function of an organ' and 'adversely affecting the function of an organ' – since 'dys' derives from the Greek 'dus' meaning 'bad'. 'Function' also has a mathematical meaning, and a simple general meaning.

The whole PACKAGE is therefore irresistible to the modern mind. It includes not only a nice meaty adjective ending in 'al' (always a good thing to get the tongue, if not the brain, around), with a specific meaning in two of the 'hard' sciences, but also a juicy Greek prefix! Let joy be unconfined! Let DYSFUNCTIONAL be unconfined as well, and let it degenerate until it is little more than a refined way of saying broken, on the blink, not working, defective.

'While we're apart we're essentially DYSFUNCTIONAL ...' The Rev Jesse Jackson, campaigning for the Democratic Presidential Nomination, reported in the *Independent*, 7.3.88)

'Divided we fall' would be more concise.

E

ECONOMIST

noun. One who scrutinises practice to see if it would work in theory.

ECONOMY OF SCALE

noun. Over-producing your manufactures to such an extent that, although your production costs inevitably increase, they are shared among a greater total of your PRODUCTS, thus bringing down the UNIT COST of each. Whether or not the public actually wishes to buy any of these beastly artefacts is an entirely unrelated matter. You have achieved an ECONOMY OF SCALE, and the Board of Directors can approach lunch with a warm glow in the corporate bosom.

In this context I always like to think of Charles Alexandre de Calonne, Louis XVI's controller-general of finances, who advocated what I feel sure the moderns would call an 'over-production of opulence' at the French court to convince the world that all was well with the French finances. From this ECONOMY OF SCALE, it can be said, the French monarchy never looked back.

ECONOMY, THE

noun. The ceaseless interaction of fear and greed.

ECUMENISM

noun. Ecclesiastical shorthand for the longing of certain Protestants to rejoin Rome on almost any terms, and the reluctance of Rome to accept them on almost any terms. A clerical dramatisation of the Young Lady of Riga, with the Protestants as the Lady, and Rome as the tiger.

EDITOR

noun. The hireling of a newspaper proprietor employed to protect the proprietor's interests, those of his shareholders, and those of his advertisers, from the drunken assaults of his loutish employees. The editor's role is not recognisable in the following self-analysis, taken from the editorial column of a national weekly.

> 'Editors are lucky because they derive from and work with journalists who are stimulating, interested and interesting people practising an under-appreciated profession and a wonderful walk of life ...' (*The Economist*, 7.2.87)

Editors on *The Economist* are not, apparently, called upon to write. Can you 'derive from' a journalist? Can you 'practise' a 'walk of life', however wonderful?

EDUCATION

noun. 1. The thrilling process of casting false pearls before real swine.
2. A task so wearisome and vile that since time immemorial it has been delegated to a despised caste of helots.

ELAPSED TIME

noun. The time taken by a computer to digest the instructions you have given it. Like civil servants and railway employees, computers are very reluctant to accept instruction, and the propitiatory patience required to lodge your message in a computer is even greater than that needed to placate its human counterparts.

EMERGENCY DEPLOYMENT READINESS EXERCISE

noun. 'We're a-comin' to git youse commie bastards, only, what with one thing and another, it seems safer not to say so in plain words.' The form of words used to explain the despatch of US troops to Honduras in March 1988, reported on BBC Radio 4 news, 11.3.88.

EMPATHY

noun. A word composed of a prefix – 'em' – and a suffix – 'pathy' – with nothing in between. It means 'the power of projecting one's personality into, and so fully understanding, the object of contemplation'.

It will be seen at once that EMPATHY embodies the two key modern aspirations – to interfere with someone or something at the same time as fully and compassionately understanding them or it. EMPATHY also embraces the seductive idea that understanding can be reached just by a psychological sleight-of-will – by 'projecting' yourself. The term is a borrowing from the German psychologists, is long overdue, and should be returned.

The moderns have let us down badly over EMPATHY. They have not displayed their normal fertility of invention. Surely a more rotund term for 'understanding by self-projection' would be 'objective subjectivism'. Or, of course, 'subjective objectivism'.

ENCOUNTER GROUP

noun. A contrivance for bringing together in controlled circumstances people so antisocial that normal gregariousness is dangerous. In a similar way the organisers of zoos gradually introduce dangerous animals they wish to mate without damaging each other.

END USER   *noun.* The lucky recipient of an end product. The hapless wretch under the inverted pyramid of commerce.

ENHANCED   *adjective.* To suggest that your product has been improved implies that it needed improvement. And yet to goad a jaded public into further acquisitions it is sometimes necessary to suggest that what is on offer is better than the last item they saw. In these circumstances the word ENHANCED is invaluable, suggesting 'strengthening' without radical alteration.

'A business gift should be both desirable and exclusive: these are the prime criteria. Accordingly we are privileged to introduce this ENHANCED range of supremely elegant pens direct from Les Stylos Pierre Cardin, Paris.' (An advertisement in *Expression!*, November 1985)

Presumably you ENHANCE a range of pens by adding more pens, or by improving the existing pens, or both, but since nothing in the copy reveals the extent of the range before ENHANCEMENT, it is difficult to determine exactly what advantage is being offered to the reader.

ENORMITY   *noun.* Properly speaking ENORMITY is 'deviation from the norm', especially deviation from moral uprightness. From this it has come to mean 'wickedness'. But because of its similarity to 'enormous' it is a common piece of modern pretentiousness to give it the meaning 'size', in spite of the fact that the OED clearly indicates 'excess in magnitude' as an incorrect use.

'The ENORMITY of the cocaine find in Southampton confirms reports ...' (*The Times*, 12.11.87)

The context makes it clear that the report refers to the size of the drug cargo discovered, and not to the delinquency of those responsible for it. There was a time when an editor of *The Times* would have had to flee the country under an assumed name after committing a solecism of such ENORMITY.

'And here we are in New York, a city still trying to come to grips with the ENORMITY of Steffi Graf's achievement.' (A commentator on the US Women's Open Tennis Championship, BBC Television, September 1988)

Steffi Graf is a strapping young Bochette, greatly expert in hitting balls over nets. In spite of the Freudian overtones of this activity only the most shrinkingly sensitive male could describe Miss Graf's achievement – which consisted of winning the Grand Slam of all the major tennis tournaments – as having 'ENORMITY'.

ENRICH

verb. How the moderns inflict ironic punishments upon their victims.

'The building is intended to ENRICH the skyline with the diversity of space and shape that the viewer could enjoy when it was dominated by Wren buildings.' (Jane Robins talking to Richard Rogers, designer of the Centre Pompidou, Paris, and the Lloyd's Building, London, in *Square Mile*, 1984)

Since 1984 the Lloyd's Building has been completed. If it was the intention to provide a substitute for Wren's delicate and elegant spires, it has not been realised. The confection of glass, steel and concrete that now juts up out of the square mile bears as much relationship to the work of Wren as a bus shelter does to the Parthenon. The comment is not only arrogant, and if made by the architect unbecomingly boastful, but also an intolerable affront to all who have watched the heartless destruction of London by modern ARCHITECTURE, grieving but powerless to resist. Rogers is not an acceptable substitute for Wren.

What he chooses to do in the privacy of the French capital is another matter, though Mr Rogers should remember that the French have the guillotine, and still sometimes use it. Both the Centre Pompidou and the Lloyd's Building suggest that Mr Rogers would be happier in sanitary engineering.

Part of the problem lies in the matter of patronage. When patronage was in the hands of the Church and the landed classes we got Wren, Hawksmoor, Gibbs, Vanbrugh, Adam and many others. Now that the whip hand is held by insurance clerks, we get Mr Rogers. I think the distinction is obvious.

There is another aspect of Mr Rogers's building, connected to patronage, that should be mentioned. It is funny. The first reaction to seeing it is to laugh. This is because, by turning the building inside out and displaying its entrails to the world, Mr Rogers has given us a glimpse of the money-makers of Lloyd's as they go about their business. Up and down they go, in little transparent lifts, looking very self-conscious and silly. Lloyd's itself has compounded this effect by stationing scarlet-liveried flunkeys in the doorway of this bizarre eruption of plumbing.

It is possible that Mr Rogers intended the comic effect, and that he stands in the long tradition of slyly mocking the patron. I hope so, but no good intentions can mitigate the horrors of this building. It commits all the cardinal sins of heroic modernism. It ignores the site. It employs tawdry materials on an oppressive scale. It boasts silly pretensions it cannot justify, like the Wren analogy. It is out of harmony even with its ghastly modern neighbours, never mind the older buildings of the City.

Rearing up out of the dusty plains of Texas a building like this would merely remind one of good old American know-how. It has no place in a European city.

EN SUITE

adjective. A term used to describe accommodation so cramped that the bath is in the bedroom.

ENTHUSE

verb. To ENTHUSE means 'to make or grow enthusiastic'. The *OED* lists it as an American back-formation from 'enthusiastic'. Such words can make their own rules, and the moderns are correspondingly likely to use them since it spares them the trouble of thinking. Besides, ENTHUSED looks enough like 'Suffused' to be ridiculous in the following context:

'Put simply we're a de-snobbed wine merchant, ENTHUSED with the joy of wine from the boardroom down.

'This no-nonsense approach has established us as the most innovative company in the field.' (An advertisement for a manager for Oddbins in *Wine* magazine, January, 1988)

An interesting feature of this advertisement is that whoever wrote it set out to disavow modern nonsense and present himself as a plain speaker.

'Forget all about the recruitment blurb about "marvellous career opportunity"', "tremendous scope for the right applicants", and "advancement potential in dominant high street chain". (It may be true, but if you're the sort to respond to dodgy doggerel, Oddbins isn't for you.)' (*Ibid.*)

Hands up whoever agrees with me that 'de-snobbed', 'ENTHUSED' and 'INNOVATIVE', all count as 'dodgy doggerel'.

ENVIRONMENT *noun.* The sum of all your surroundings. A word now used so all-embracingly that it has lost any precise meaning. The British government actually boasts a Department of the ENVIRONMENT, a portfolio of immense latitude, like the Ministry of Truth in *1984*. Here is a more domestic use of ENVIRONMENT:

'Fourteen foot floor to ceiling heights ... will be complemented by appropriate heating and ventilation to ensure a comfortable and controlled working ENVIRONMENT.' (J. Scott Lowry, chief ARCHITECT of the Canary Wharf development project in London's docklands, writing in *Property Now*, Summer 1987)

Everything from 'appropriate' to 'ENVIRONMENT' could be reduced to 'air conditioning'. Mr Lowry is offering no more than 'air conditioned offices'.

'Air conditioning' is itself a piece of nonsense. The grand-sounding word 'conditioning' refers merely to the process of heating or cooling, or sometimes filtering, the air. 'Conditioning' suggests that the air is in some way being improved. 'Hair conditioner' relies on the same suggestion – vainly, since hair is dead, and beyond the help of even the most active 'conditioning agent'.

The ENVIRONMENT stretches from the ionosphere to the bottom of the Marianas Trench. CONSCIOUSNESS of the ENVIRONMENT is no longer the preserve of the CONSERVATIONIST middle classes. If the existence of a Department of the ENVIRONMENT did not sound a warning bell in your head, here surely is the clinching evidence that the ENVIRONMENT is not what it seems:

'NO PERCH bird control. Peter Cox. ENVIRONMENT services.' (Sign painted on the side of a van, seen in the City of London, March 1988)

Roosting space in the Square Mile is very limited, and the feather-brained are constantly jostling the feather-clad. So long as he is careful to distinguish one from the other, Mr Cox has the opportunity to provide an ENVIRONMENT service of inestimable value.

EPISTEMOLOGICAL   *adjective.* Exhibiting the quality of knowing how to know.

EQUAL OPPORTUNITIES   *noun.* Jobs for all – saving those, of course, who do not belong to a trade union.

The term EQUAL OPPORTUNITIES is POSITIVE DISCRIMINATION in Liberal clothing. It is very worthy. So worthy that here is an example of one of the modern elect actually admitting fallibility:

'Shelter *strives to be* an EQUAL OPPORTUNITIES employer ...' (Advertisement by Shelter in *The Times*, 27.1.88 [my italics])

Here is another example from the even more sheltered world of academe:

'If you are trying to be serious about being an EQUAL OPPORTUNITIES employer you have to make that clear in ways that seem trivial on one level.' (Dr Joan Whitehead, lecturer in Educational Psychology at Cambridge University, reported in the *Independent*, 31.10.88., speaking of the University's decision to rewrite the Univerity Statutes 'in gender free terms'. In other words using 'she' as well as 'he' whenever the third person singular pronoun crops up)

The fact that something *seems* trivial on one level, does not preclude its actually *being* trivial on all levels.

On the other hand, perhaps it is suitable for the bluestockings of Cambridge to be burning their bras, in view of the age-old jibe that a Combination Room is no more than the unhappy marriage of a vestry and a pantry.

(See MEANINGFUL.)

EQUITATION   *noun.* The art and science by which 180 lbs of bone and muscle subdue 1,000 lbs of the same, often equipped with a better brain. See also Death Wish, Suicidal Tendencies and Dutch Courage.

ERGONOMICS   *noun.* The science that seeks to perfect the human frame's adaption to the needs of the treadmill.

'An efficient ERGONOMICALLY designed PC workstation for professional users.' (Advertisement for the Holltec PC workstation, *Accountancy*, June, 1987)

In this instance 'ERGONOMICALLY designed' means 'designed to deprive you of any excuse for leaving your post'.

ESCALATION   *noun.* The propensity of wars to get worse before they get better.

ETHICS

noun. An academic discipline invented by the Americans. Like Civics, but without its heavy moral overtones.

ETHNIC

adjective. Coloured. ETHNIC minorities. ETHNIC prints. ETHNIC handbags – all have only one thing in common: colour. (See BLACK.)

ETHNOCENTRIC

adjective. Obsessed with coloured prints, handbags, beads, etc.

EURO

adjective. An abbreviation of 'European', usually coupled with a noun to designate some unwanted project that will benefit only a few bankers and bureaucrats – EUROtunnel, EURObond, EUROcheque.

The western Europeans, shorn of their colonial empires, have been reduced to robbing each other. The checks and balances required to ensure that each nation gets its hand well and truly into the till have given rise to an epic of bureaucracy. The old system of fighting for the spoils was much better, and gave even the Germans the opportunity to excel from time to time.

EURO is a highly-characteristic late 20th-century coinage: cheap, cheery, and ugly both to the ear and eye. It invariably denotes something extravagant, vulgar and useless – like EURO MP.

Besides, if we must have a two-syllable alternative to European, should it not be Eurine?

EURO-COMMUNIST

noun. A communist who is half European. Where the other half of his allegiance lies is a matter between him and his KGB control.

ELITISM

noun. Any indication, however tiny, that one does not hold mankind to be of invariable sameness.

> ' ... there is little comfort for them in Kenneth Baker's ELITIST middle-class proposals.' (A correspondent to the BBC4 programme *Today*, 22.3.88., speaking of modern education and the high incidence of illiteracy)

I don't question that Mr Baker's proposals are comfortless, but I find difficulty in recognising the middle classes in their new role as an elite.

EVENT

noun. What is an EVENT? 'Anything that happens' seems to be the answer, and EVENT has become the serious 1980s equivalent of the flippant 'happening' of the sixties.

> 'If words are your business then Time Out Live is your EVENT. For four days in May we can introduce you to an audience passionate about print. We know because they are *Time Out* readers. Unlike book fairs, Time Out Live will be interactive, inviting participation at every level.' (Advertisement in *Time Out*, 3.2.88)

Are you sure you want to meet someone passionate about print? It is revealing that only when the EVENT is compared with a book fair does it become clear what the EVENT is about.

But it is just this vagueness, combined with the suggestion of action, that makes the word EVENT so valuable to the modern mind.

'Interactive' is rather jolly too, joining PROACTIVE and 'reactive' in the random activity stakes.

The Three-Day EVENT (see EQUI-

TATION) looms in stark contrast to Time Out Live. Here you will encounter an audience not passionate about print, but hysterical about horses. 'Interactivity' there is in plenty, especially when a horse wisely declines to surmount one of the obstacles placed in its path. The Three-Day EVENT occupies a very special place in British society. In the past the sting of inequality was softened by EVENTS like officers' serving their men's dinners on Christmas Day. Nowadays the many-headed can attend a Three-Day EVENT and witness members of the Royal House being ducked.

EXECUTIVE

noun. A functionary in business and industry whose activities correspond to those of the drone in a beehive. Without a queen on which to focus his attentions, however, he is reduced to importuning secretaries. An EXECUTIVE is often UPWARDLY MOBILE, and some companies refer to their EXECUTIVES as 'officers', in a sad attempt to borrow what little social allure still attaches to the Queen's Commission.

adjective. A designation applied to cars, male cosmetics, and leather goods, to attract the custom of such wretches and outcasts as aspire to EXECUTIVE status.

EXFILTRATION

noun. Pentagonese for retreat, or getting the hell out.

EXIT MULTIPLE

noun. Profit. The number of times your investment has multiplied itself by the moment you cannily decide to get the hell out.

EXPENSES

noun. A polite fiction for the desperate stratagems adopted by journalists to eke out their miserable salaries.

EXPERIENTIAL DEPRIVATION

noun. Depriving living creatures of their normal surroundings and thwarting their normal instincts in the capricious interests of experiment.

EXPERT

noun. Any source or authority too insignificant for a journalist to mention by name.

The very last thing that EXPERTS in this category have is any sort of expertise. Frequently they are 'expert' in a subject requiring only the most rudimentary skills. They are deployed as EXPERTS solely to lend weight to the journalist's report.

EXPONENTIAL

adjective. Pertaining to unknown quantities and variables. In mathematics, as a noun, it means 'an EXPONENTIAL quantity or function, specifically the Napierian base *e* raised to the power denoted by the variable.'

Obscure stuff, but mathematicians will have their fun, and since EXPONENTIAL is a long and not very graceful word, it seems only fair to let them keep it.

But it is not to be. EXPONENTIAL exercises an irresistible fascination over the sub-intelligentsia, and it is used with frivolous abandon in contexts where more familiar words would do just a well.

'On a second level, medical practice sponsors sickness by reinforcing a morbid society that not only industrially preserves its defectives, but also EXPONENTIALLY breeds demand for the patient role.' (Father Ivan Illich, *Medical Nemesis*, Calder & Boyars, 1975)

I think he means 'proportionally', but one cannot be sure because Father Illich is a Grand Master of Modern Nonsense. He specialises in suggesting that established institutions – medicine, schooling – are of no value, and probably dangerous as well. In *Medical Nemesis* he tries to convince his readers that the practice of medicine represents a 'major threat to health'. Since he gives smallpox, syphilis and cholera as examples of other 'threats to health', he naturally fails to make his case, but in trying he runs his head into the noose of tendentious terminology again and again, and the passage quoted is significant in several respects.

'Medical practice sponsors sickness' suggests active participation in encouraging sickness, but in fact Illich means only that medical practice sometimes exacerbates sickness. The word 'reinforcing' is deployed in the same way to suggest that medical practice plays an active role in buttressing some form of malpractice. It is difficult to know if Father Illich means 'morbid' in its medical sense of 'indicative of disease', or in its popular sense of 'unwholesome'. Either way it can hardly describe a whole society. 'Industrially preserves its defectives' may mean 'keeps the sick on their feet with drugs and surgery'. 'EXPONENTIALLY' to 'role' means 'to the same extent encourages people to see themselves as patients'. (Note the borrowing from economics – 'demand', as in 'supply and demand' – to make the whole process sound automatic, inevitable, and subject to grand laws of which only Father Illich and his like are initiates.)

One could go through all Father Illich's work word by word, giving instances of where he uses terminology in this slanted way. He studied theology under the Gregorians in Rome, and no doubt this has influenced his cast of mind. To some extent choice of vocabulary is an instinctive matter, and all writers are guilty of using coloured terminology, but in Father Illich the disease seems chronic and endemic.

We shall be returning to Father Illich, but before we leave him for the nonce, here is another example of his prose style:

> 'By using the Greek term I want to emphasise that the corresponding CONCEPT does not fit in with the explanatory paradigm now offered by engineers, therapists and IDEOLOGUES for the snowballing diseconomies, disutilities and COUNTER INITIATIVE behaviour of large systems. By invoking myths and ancestral gods it should be clear that my framework for analysis of the current breakdown of medicine is foreign to any industrially determined logic and ethos.' (*Ibid.*)

I think the beginning of the last sentence should read: 'It should be clear from my having invoked myths and ancestral gods ...'

EXTRA

adjective. Sometimes ADDED. Any quantity above the legal minimum of the essential ingredients of your PRODUCT. The really cunning manufacturer makes no mention of the actual components of his PRODUCT, but boasts of added abstractions – like extra value – whose presence or absence cannot be detected. See VALUE ADDED TAX.

F

FABULOUS

adjective. All too true, as in your daughter saying: 'There's this FABULOUS man!'

FACILITY

noun. A word used by bureaucrats to name a service that can be wrung out of them only with the greatest difficulty. As in 'overdraft FACILITY'. (See STAND-BY CREDIT FACILITY)

FAILSOFT

noun. One of the functions in a computer of such exquisite delicacy that it can sense the approach of mechanical breakdown, and firmly but discreetly switch itself off. All marriages should be fitted with a FAILSOFT mode (or FACILITY).

FALSE CON-SCIOUSNESS

noun. A term used by MARXISTS to indicate any notion of 'the self' that does not follow the class lines indicated by Marx. In other words, if your ideas and aspirations do not exactly reflect your position in the process of production, you are the victim of FALSE CONSCIOUS-NESS, almost certainly inflict- ed on you by a 'system'.

Such a term is a boon to the intolerant puritans of the left, for whom it has provided an 'analytical tool' with which to belabour anyone who steps out of line. If you are a labourer, but vote Tory; if you are a sewage disposal operative, but hanker after a small house with a garden; if you in any way lack revolutionary consciousness – then you are guilty of FALSE CONSCIOUSNESS.

The one-eyed narrowness of this view should convince any doubters that MARXISTS are interested in ideas and not people, in spite of their protestations to the contrary. And ideas are usually baneful, and always ridiculous – even when parading as CONCEPTS.

For some reason the term FALSE CONSCIOUSNESS is not used to describe members of the intelligentsia who ape what they take to be proletarian manners and morals.

FAMILY

noun. A mixture of human temperaments so volatile and explosive that it is frequently dignified with the adjective 'nuclear'.

FASCISM

noun. Failure to keep your feet in the shifting sands of left-wing orthodoxy.

FASCIST and FASCISM are less popular as terms of abuse than they were in the 60s and 70s, but they are still widely used to castigate anyone who disagrees with the strident left. The practices of FASCISM – intimidating opponents, breaking up meetings, and so forth – are now the property of the far left themselves, and those they castigate are usually woolly-headed old goody-goodies who actually believe in outmoded stuff like FREE SPEECH.

If the left restricted their use of FASCISM to the behaviour of genuine authoritarians, they would be on strong ground, since the word derives from the bundle of rods carried by the lictors of ancient Rome to whack the plebs out of the way when the patricians wanted a clear road. But they usually employ the term about people who wouldn't dream of having servants – never mind servants empowered to whack

people. Their confusion of thought is clearly indicated by the fact that LIBERTARIANISM is rapidly supplanting FASCISM in their demonology.
(See DIRECT MASS DEMOCRACY and REPRESSIVE TOLERANCE)

FASHION

noun. A conspiracy of decrepit harridans and embittered homosexuals to cloak the charms of young women in shapeless rags.

FAST

adjective. Not actually stationary.

> 'Stand well clear of the platform. FAST train approaching.' (An announcement frequently to be heard at London Bridge Station)

It heralds the arrival of a train which has only just managed to overcome the inertia of its own mass, and which creeps along the platform in little spasmodic jerks, like a glacier inching down an Alpine valley. Eventually it clears the platform, leaving the waiting passengers frozen in imitative immobility, and departs towards Kent, but with no obvious enthusiasm.

These trains are invariably empty.

British Rail, however, is not content with this revision of the word FAST. It doesn't go far enough.

> 'Charing Cross train. Charing Cross train. FAST to Waterloo East and Charing Cross!' (A litany sent up from many suburban railway stations at about 0800 hours, like the muezzin calling the faithful to prayer)

No passenger should suppose that he will be whisked smoothly and swiftly to his destination. FAST means only that it doesn't stop *at any other station.* Beyond this mild restriction it is free to stop anywhere, and does, sometimes in places so desolate that it seems impossible that they support life, even of the rudimentary kind that travels by British Rail Network South East.

FEEDBACK

noun. The capacity of a computer to chew its cud.

> 'I will designate this self-reinforcing loop of NEGATIVE institutional FEEDBACK by its classical Greek equivalent and call it medical nemesis.' (Father Ivan Illich, *Medical Nemesis*, Calder & Boyars, 1975)

'Self-reinforcing loop of NEGATIVE institutional FEEDBACK' is a very long way of saying 'retributive justice', the meaning of NEMESIS most likely to suit Father Illich's meaning here. He is referring to the tendency of the practice of medicine to cause further illness – by cross-infection, drug reactions, the need for surgical after care, and so on. Why such a phenomenon should be 'retributive justice' is not immediately obvious to a mind that has not studied theology. Father Illich seems to think that the practice of medicine is impious, and therefore invites divine retribution.

FEMINIST

noun. One who kicks against the pricks.

FIGHTER

noun. A youth, insufficiently disciplined or battle-hardened to be called a soldier, upon whom the vagaries of power politics have conferred an automatic weapon. His chief function is to fire this in front of TELEVISION cameras, but only rarely, alas, at them. (Freedom FIGHTER, Islamic FIGHTER, PLO FIGHTER.)

FLAIR

noun. The quality exhibited by CREATIVE staff, usually after lunch.

'We require an experienced Art Director who will exercise CREATIVE FLAIR on our large and expanding PRODUCT range.' (Advertisement by Pickwick International in *The Times*, 27.1.88)

FLEXIBLE

adjective. Wanting precision.

'The course content is FLEXIBLE.' (*The Plain English Training Course*, published by the Plain English Campaign)

So FLEXIBLE that it includes an introduction entitled 'Reasons for a Plain English Approach'. Why not 'The Need for Plain English'?

For advocates of Plain English, the campaign's founders, Chrissie Maher and Martin Cutts, publish some curiously flat and uninteresting prose. It can certainly be called plain. The course in question is a '1-day, IN-HOUSE course' which undertakes to make 'course members' into 'constructive critics' of language. 'We've Discovered the Ultimate Word Processors' they declare, referring to the human brain cell which, as represented in their own heads, will solve all their clients' problems.

The fact is that in their assault on official jargon, the Plain English Campaigners have fallen into the trap of over-familiarity. For instance they now 'head' a 'team' of twelve. In Plain English, they employ twelve people. Chrissie Maher founded a newspaper 'specifically designed for people with reading difficulties'. That is not Plain English.

What they need is a less FLEXIBLE approach.

FLOWCHART

noun. An attempt to depict graphically the abstract beauties of a computer programme. This, of course, is impossible, like trying to render the glory of God in paint or stone, but many worthy efforts are made. It is important that coloured lines should project themselves purposefully through thick bars labelled 'mode' and 'memory map', but above all there must be regular 'process boxes' and 'decision lozenges'. These images, like the arrows on a staff officer's map, bear more relation to what is intended than to what happens, but, like the staff officer's map, they are important in keeping idle hands employed that might otherwise make irreparable mischief.

FOOD SOPHISTICATION

noun. Adulteration. Adding foreign elements to food for motives of profit. (See ADDITIVES). The use of the word 'sophistication' in this context is almost poignantly delicate. It does, of course, mean adulteration. It also means 'sophistry' or 'the employment of specious fallacies'. On top of that it has its modern, debased meaning of smartness, worldliness and savoir-faire. It is difficult to know which of these meanings was uppermost in the minds of the food biz moguls and their advertising jargonauts when they hit on this deliciously ambiguous phrase.

FORWARD PLANNING/ CONTINGENCY PLANNING

noun. Planning for those who do not really understand planning, and need to be reminded that plans are laid for the future, against possible happenings.

FREE SPEECH

noun. 1. A condition in society that automatically confers station and influence on those most free in their speech.
2. The inability to silence your opponent.

FREE WORLD

noun. That part of the world in which mankind's sufferings may be observed, broadcast and dwelt upon with the greatest relish. (See DEVELOPING and LDCs.)

FRESH

adjective. Canned or frozen. Produce straight from the garden or field that is *not* fresh, being contaminated by earth, rain, sunshine and other filthy pollutants.

FRINGE THEATRE

noun. The amateur dramatics of the left.

FUCK

Verb and *noun.* To swive, couple, mount or serve. Perhaps the most widely-understood English word, often referred to as Anglo-Saxon. Every dictionary I have consulted, however, has been evasive about the derivation of this word, mumbling feebly about early English and German.

Since I am writing a Dictionary of Nonsense, I have no hesitation in offering the following derivation, for which I have no shred of evidence.

At some point in English-speaking history – probably under the Commonwealth or in Puritan New England – it was actually against the law to have extra-marital hoggins. The ensuing avalanche of prosecutions so overwhelmed the courts that the idle scriveners, instead of writing out in full 'For Unlawful Carnal Knowledge', scribbled instead the acronym F.U.C.K. on each transcript of the charges.

Any takers?

FUNDAMENTALIST

noun. A religious extremist so stupid that even the simple strictures of the Prophet Mohammed are beyond his comprehension, for which reason he is forced back on still-more-basic propositions. One who mistakes the atavistic promptings of his self-esteem for Holy Writ.

There are also Christian FUNDA-MENTALISTS who suffer from a NOR-MAL READING AGE problem and have not got beyond the Book of Genesis.

FUTURISTIC

adjective. The quality of any more-than-usually hideous building or machine. Worse than modern: even worse than contemporary.

'TO TEST THE STRENGTH OF THE WORLD'S MOST FUTURISTIC BANK, WE ATTACKED IT WITH A WORLD WAR II FIGHTER. Construct-ing one of the world's most INNO-VATIVE glass and steel buildings would be challenge enough for most, but Wimpey had to build it in one of the world's most notorious typhoon areas – Hong Kong.' (An advertisement placed by Wimpey in the *Independent* 22.11.88)

Hong Kong is a ghastly place, where all the most boring elements of European materialism mingle freely with the dullest aspects of Oriental cupidity, but even Hong Kong doesn't deserve the scale of archi-tectural FUTURISM it has suffered.

The advertisement went on to describe how, to test the resilience of the glass structure, Wimpey parked a US Navy Corsair next to it and revved-up the propeller.

This generated sufficiently gusty condi-tions to satisfy them about the stability of their frightful erection. The most depress-ing thing about modern buildings is that they are structurally strong, and will continue to affront the eye long after they have become about as FUTURISTIC as wattle and daub.

G

GAYS

noun. Male homosexuals. Lesbian women are sometimes referred to as Gay Women, but GAYS as a plural noun seems to mean men. Even before the onslaught of AIDS, homosexuals were always a pretty lugubrious lot, and now anything less gay than the GAY community can hardly be imagined.

'Runcie backs bishops over GAYS.' (Headline in *The Times*, 20.12.87)

Not long ago this headline would have been quite incomprehensible. Even now it sounds like a piece of heartlessly bad driving. There was a time when *The Times* would not have printed sloppy journalese like 'backs' and 'over', never mind GAYS, but *The Times*, like the Anglican Church, is in decline.

The headline referred to the Archbishop of Canterbury, Dr Robert Runcie, giving support to the view expressed by some of his bishops that practising homosexuals should not be ordained to the priesthood. Celibate homosexuals, however, were another matter, and not necessarily barred from ordination. But if *practising* GAYS are universally gloomy, can *celibate* GAYS be relied on not to sink into the sin of despair?

GENETIC ENGINEERING

noun. The art of getting inside jeans.

103

GENTLEMAN

noun. One who cultivates a liberality of manner to match a liberality of means. A British stereotype, playing the same part in the national morality play as the western gunslinger in the American version. Both are sparing of syllables and lavish with lead.

GENTRIFICATION

noun. The invasion of working-class areas by middle-class house buyers. At no point does anyone connected with what used to be called the Gentry take part in these transactions.

GENUINITY

noun. Somewhere between genuineness and fatuity. Almost as good as AUTHENTICITY.

'This wine has not been pasteurised and like all natural wines it may develop, with time, a sediment which is the sign of the GENUINITY and high quality of the product.' (The wording of a label displayed on Signor Guerrieri Rizzardi's bottles of Soave Classico)

My dear Watson, it is sedimentary.

GLOBAL

adjective. Embracing a whole world, however limited.

' ... the man who, starting with nothing except his courage, foresight, ingenuity and driving energy, fought his way to the pinnacle of GLOBAL success.'

Who can this be? The President of the United States? The Soviet head of state? Who else can claim to occupy *the* pinnacle of GLOBAL success?

Well, it is neither of these. It is our own beloved Robert Maxwell, publisher and newspaper proprietor, as described in a book society blurb for his authorised biography by Joe Haines. Mr Maxwell's career is fraught with varied incident, and his position is an enviable one. But the pinnacle of GLOBAL success? Hardly.

The blurb writer does not accept this restricted interpretation of GLOBAL, and indeed the word seems to transfix him. Here is the unhappy man again, on the same subject:

'Today he is a GLOBAL media entrepreneur ...'

GOOD NEWS BIBLE   *noun.* An attempt to make the word of God accessible to the victims of COMPREHENSIVE EDUCATION. Making The Word half a word.

'Every effort has been made to use language that is natural, clear, simple and unambiguous.' (Preface to *The Good News Bible* [GNB], The Bible Societies/Collins, 1976)

Simple the language certainly is. Natural to whom? Clear and unambiguous it cannot be, any more than the Authorised Version is, because the texts are old, obscure and of dubious provenance.

There are a number of reasons for the GNB's poor comparison with the Authorised Version, and the first is that it was written in the twentieth century. Everywhere in the GNB you encounter failures of nerve. Confronted with a vivid image, the translators shy away from it, or blur it. The reason is not far to seek. The King James translators, pausing from their labours and looking out of the window, saw a world order which was obviously divinely ordained. They saw that robins always mated with other robins and produced further robins. They saw the seasons come round in an appointed pattern. They saw an order, which clearly implied an organiser, and they were therefore in close sympathy with the imagery of the original texts.

The moderns, raising their haggard faces from their desks, enjoy no such certainty. They do not see robins. They see volatile and capricious bundles of DNA that not long ago were pre-robins, and shortly will be post-robins. They see not ordered seasons, but a mad career towards the next ice age. They see the evidence of a universe so huge and chaotic that it exceeds the power of the human imagination to encompass it. The natural world is not a stable source of unchanging metaphor, but a dangerous quicksand. They are therefore out of tune with the certainties of the Old and New Testaments, and shy away from any vocabulary that is strong and arresting.

'The Bible is not simply great literature to be admired and revered; it is GOOD NEWS for all people everywhere ... ' (*Ibid.*)

Is it no more than GOOD NEWS? Is it not the Truth, the Light and the Life? GOOD NEWS has all the hallmarks of Modern Nonsense. It is cheery, vapid and inaccurate. It is taken from 'gospel', which is supposed to derive from 'godspel', old Engish for good tidings. But the Gospels comprise only part of the Bible, and there is much in the rest of the Bible that cannot possibly be described as Good Tidings – especially if you happened to be an Israelite.

Nor should they be in such a hurry to dismiss the point about great literature. The Authorised Version is great literature *because* it reflects the BELIEF of the authors and translators. If your language fails to match the overpowering sensation of BELIEF, your words will fall flat, and you will end up with egg on your faith.

The differences between the GNB and the Authorised Version also stem from a conceit on the part of the GNB translators.

> 'After ascertaining as accurately as possible the meaning of the original, the translators' next task was to express the meaning in a manner and form easily understood by the readers.' (*Ibid.*)

In other words they set out to condescend to an imagined audience, partly out of contempt for the audience, and partly out of a lack of confidence in their PRODUCT, which was assumed to need sweetening like a bitter pill.

The Authorised Version suffers neither from arrogance nor a lack of confidence, and it successfully spread The Word for three and a half centuries.

During these years any Englishman could hear the words of the Authorised Version or the Book of Common Prayer in any church at least once a week and often daily. They formed the basis of his religious education at home and at school, and the rhythms and imagery of the Authorised Version formed the background of any educated man's command of prose and verse. The Anglican Church was the guardian of one of the great wells of English undefiled.

Now look how they have defiled it. The Authorised Version is rarely heard, and in its place is found one of the modern translations, of which the Good News Bible is infinitely the worst. Let us begin at the beginning.

'In the beginning God created the heaven and the earth.' Genesis 1.1. Authorised Version.

'In the beginning, when God created the universe ...' Genesis 1.1. GNB.

Whatever happened to 'heaven'? Certainly 'the heavens' means the sky, and therefore the universe of galaxies and what-not that we now know to be swirling about out there (see BIG BANG), but surely the Authorised Version means 'heaven' in the theological sense as well? The Authorised Version is not difficult to understand. Why have 'heaven and earth' become 'universe'? I don't think the man who made this alteration feels much at home with the idea of 'heaven'.

And the whales, damnit! Look what they've done to the whales!

'And God created great whales, and every living creature that moveth ...' Genesis 1.21, Authorised Version.

'So God created the great sea monsters, all kinds of creatures that live in the water ...' *Ib*. GNB.

Well, every living creature moveth all right, but not the prose of the GNB translators. The rhythm of the first extract is entirely lost in the second, and what is gained by calling the whales 'sea monsters'? As we shall see, it is a lack of precision in imagery and no feeling for the rhythms of English that make the GNB so flat and uninspiring. But it is also bedevilled by the banality of its ideas, as if everything were happening in a sociology seminar for under-achievers.

'And his soul clave unto Dinah the daughter of Jacob, and he loved the damsel, and spake kindly unto the damsel.' Genesis 34.2/3. Authorised Version.

'But he found the girl so attractive that he fell in love with her and tried to win her affection.' *Ib*. GNB.

Anyone who has fallen suddenly in love will recognise the force and accuracy of 'his soul clave unto Dinah', however old-fashioned the diction may sound. The second attempt — 'he found the girl so attractive that he fell in love with her' — is without any power of imagery.

On to the second Book of Samuel. Here we meet King David, prostrated with grief by the death of Saul and Jonathan. He has torn his clothes, mourned, fasted, and struck down Saul's assassin. In this emotional state he gives vent to his great outpouring:

'The beauty of Israel is slain upon thy high places: how are the mighty fallen!

Tell it not in Gath, publish it not in the streets of Askelon; lest the daughters of the Philistines rejoice, lest the daughters of the uncircumcised triumph.

Ye mountains of Gilboa, let there be no dew, neither let there be rain, upon you, nor fields of offerings: for there the shield of the mighty is vilely cast away; the shield of Saul, as though he had not been annointed with oil.

From the blood of the slain, from the fat of the mighty, the bow of Jonathan turned not back, and the sword of Saul returned not empty.

Saul and Jonathan were lovely and pleasant in their lives, and in their death they were not divided: they were swifter than eagles, they were stronger than lions.

Ye daughters of Israel, weep over Saul, who clothed you in scarlet, with other delights, who put ornaments of gold upon your apparel.

How are the mighty fallen in the midst of battle! O Jonathan, thou wast slain in thine high places.

I am distressed for thee my brother Jonathan: very pleasant hast thou been unto me: thy love to me was wonderful, passing the love of women.

How are the mighty fallen, and the weapons of war perished.' (2 Samuel 1, 19-27. Authorised Version)

I do not think it fanciful to suggest that David's grief is communicated to us directly by this magnificent declamatory passage, even across so many centuries, and in spite of the use of words – 'lovely', 'pleasant' – which sound odd to the modern ear in this context.

Can the Anglican churchgoer any longer share King David's sorrow? Only if he has superhuman powers of imagination, because this is what he is likely to hear:

'On the hills of Israel our leaders are dead! The bravest of our soldiers have fallen!

Do not announce it in Gath or in the streets of Askelon. Do no make the women of Phillistia glad; do not let the daughters of the pagans rejoice.

May no rain or dew fall on Gilboa's hills; may its fields be always barren! For the shields of the brave lie there in disgrace; the shield of Saul is no longer polished with oil.

Jonathan's bow was deadly, the sword of Saul was merciless, striking down the mighty, killing the enemy.

Saul and Jonathan, so wonderful and dear; together in life, together in death; swifter than eagles, stronger than lions.

Women of Israel, mourn for Saul! He clothed you in rich scarlet dresses and adorned you with jewels and gold.

The brave soldiers have fallen, they were killed in battle. Jonathan lies dead in the hills.

I grieve for you my brother Jonathan; how dear you were to me! How wonderful was your love for me, better even than the love of women.

The brave soldiers have fallen, their weapons abandoned and useless.' (*Ibid.* GNB)

This is not the great warrior King of Israel trumpeting out his loss. It sounds more like a modern bishop admonishing a confirmation class for prejudice towards GAYS, BLACKS and women. The note of keening of personal loss has been abandoned. Saul and Jonathan – 'the beauty of Israel' – have become 'our leaders'. 'The mighty' have become 'brave soldiers'. The imperatives 'Tell it not' and 'publish it not' have become 'do not announce it' and 'do not let'. The outburst, 'O Jonathan, though wast slain in thine high places' has been flattened into 'Jonathan lies dead in the hills'.

Bah! Handless oafs! Let us press on to poor old Job.

Everything that happens to Job arises out of what must be described as a bet between Satan and God. Job bears his sufferings heroically, and when he does at last let out a bleat, he gets the biggest earful in history. First, here is Job reaffirming his faith in words which are known throughout the English speaking world as a declaration of faith in adversity.

'O that my words were now written! O that they were printed in a book!

That they were graven with an iron pen and lead in the rock for ever!

For I know that my redeemer liveth, and that he shall stand at the latter day upon the earth:' (Job 19, 23-25. Authorised Version)

Now for a trip down Banality Lane.

'How I wish that someone would remember my words and record them in a book!
Or with a chisel carve my words in stone and write them so that they would last for ever.
But I know there is someone in heaven who will come at last to my defence.' (*Ibid.* GNB)

Later Job's faith becomes almost as feeble as it sounds in the GNB. After a few chapters of warm-up reproof from Elihu, Jahweh himself wades in. When you come to the GNB version, remember that this is the terrible, wrathful God of Israel reminding his long-suffering servant Job of the paltriness of Job's impiety, and of the overwhelming, all-embracing might of God.

'Then the Lord answered Job out of the whirlwind and said.
Who is it that darkeneth counsel by words without knowledge?
Gird up now thy loins like a man; for I will demand of thee, and answer thou me.
Where wast thou when I laid the foundations of the earth? declare, if thou hast understanding.
Who hath laid the measures thereof, if thou knowest? or who hath stretched the line upon it?
Whereupon are the foundations

thereof fastened? Or who laid the cornerstone thereof;
When the morning stars sang together, and all the sons of God shouted for joy?' (Job 38, 1-7, Authorised Version)

'Then out of the storm the Lord spoke to Job.
Who are you to question my wisdom with your ignorant empty words?
Stand up now like a man and answer the questions I ask you.
Where were you when I made the world? If you know so much, tell me about it.
Who decided how large it would be? Who stretched the measuring line over it? Do you know all the answers?
What holds up the pillars that support the earth? Who laid the corner stone of the world?
In the dawn of that day the stars sang together, and the heavenly beings shouted for joy.' (*Ibid.* GNB)

God has become a tetchy schoolmaster. 'Do you know all the answers?' is a piece of slangy bathos. 'Heavenly beings' is a revealing modern evasion. It wouldn't do to be too precise about the inhabitants of heaven, be they Sons of God or angels.

I cannot bring myself to tell you what has happened to the warhorse that saith Ha, ha; among the trumpets, and as for Leviathan (see MEGAFORM), 'whose breath kindleth coals', now 'his breath starts fires burning.'

Do the moderns have any better luck with the New Testament? Surely they will feel more at home with St Paul's methods of argument? Won't they?

'Though I speak with the tongues of men and of angels, and have not charity, I am become as sounding brass, or a tinkling cymbal.' (1 Corinthians 13, 1. Authorised Version).

'I may be able to speak the languages of men and even of angels, but if I have no love, my speech is no more than a noisy gong or clanging bell.' (*Ibid*. GNB)

'O death, where is thy sting? O grave, where is thy victory?' (*Ibid*. 15,55. Authorised Version)

'Where, death, is your victory? Where, death, is your power to hurt?' (*Ibid*. GNB)

I have not been unfairly selective. On almost every page of the GNB there is an example of resounding bathos. Let the other churches do as they please. There was no need for the Church of England to adopt any of the new translations, and certainly no need to abandon the Book of Common Prayer. The reason given, that more people would come to church if the words and forms of worship were 'modern', has proved quite false. The present bench of bishops does not seem likely to yield a candidate for the See of Canterbury with the taste or courage to restore their lost heritage to the English. When the present incumbent chucks in the towel, I urge Her Majesty's advisers to some CREATIVE thinking.

GOURMET *noun*. One who puts his mouth where his money is.

GRASS ROOTS *noun*. The level of the beasts of the field, to which POLITICIANS frequently boast of lowering themselves.

'Greens prepare to woo GRASS ROOTS Liberals.' (Headline in the *Independent*, 18.9.87)

Apart from the absurd picture conjured up, there is a disconcerting echo of the parade ground here. 'Stand by your Liberals! Prepare to woo! Wait for it! Wait for it! On the word of command ... WOO!'

GREY AREAS

noun. The Boers, for so long given to seeing problems in black and white, have rather late in the day admitted an intermediate shade to their view of life. GREY AREAS are white districts where black and coloured people have settled in defiance of the Boers' strict rules, but in such numbers that nothing can be done about it. Since this is approximately the chromatic reverse of what happened when the Dutch first arrived among the Hottentots of the Cape, there is a certain natural justice to it.

'Pretoria recognises GREY AREAS'. (A headline in the *Independent*, 18.9.87).

More generally, a GREY AREA indicates any subject on which the speaker or writer is incompletely informed.

GROWTH AREAS

noun. Those ever-contracting sectors of the economy in which it is possible to make a profit.

H

HANDS ON

adjective. Descriptive of the stance of any truly dynamic, SELF-STARTING EXECUTIVE. In touch. Up front. Of high CONSCIOUSNESS. In touch with the main issues. Directly influencing the DECISION-MAKING PROCESS.

'Because technology has become increasingly important, you require service from practitioners who have HANDS ON experience.' (*Proven Professionals*, a brochure advertising the services of Touche Ross, a 'BROAD BASED Professional Services Firm')

'Practical experience' would probably do as well.

HAPPY HOUR

noun. A brief interval that precedes an unhappy 23 hours.

HARD-LINE

adjective. Too stupid to think of alternatives, too obstinate to compromise.

HAWK

noun. Any person advocating intransigent policies. HAWKS (and Doves) were first identified in the Pentagon and Congress during the Cuban crisis. Since then both species have proliferated, and have found many an ecological niche to exploit. A HAWK is not tied to any party, creed or nation, and may crop up anywhere. The Kremlin, for instance, is plentifully supplied with HAWKS. Here is a sub-species from southern Africa:

116

'Mbeki rally banned as Pretoria HAWKS hit at release policy.' (*The Times*, 10.12.87)

The people referred to are members of the South African security forces. Anything less like a HAWK than a Boer general would be hard to picture. From Piet Retief onwards, none of them has had the figure to suggest aerobatics. But HAWK has become a convenient shorthand for head-line writers and other non-thinkers, and General van der Merwe and Mynheer Adriaan Vlok (the villains of this piece) must be content to rub shoulders with their fellow intransigents in Washington, the Kremlin, the Knesset, the Vatican, and numerous other seats of government.

To use the word HAWK to indicate such people is a gross slander on birds of exquisite evolutionary refinement and deli-cate appetites.

HEAD-UP

verb. 'To HEAD-UP' – to strike the heroic posture of an American company president in the van of a corporate attack. The characteristic attitude of corporate leader-ship. What EXECUTIVES are said to do by those who can't bear the overtones of work in 'manage', nor the ELITIST echoes of 'lead'.

HEALTH

noun. Chronic disease, as in 'Department of Health', 'Health Care'.

HEAVY-KNIT

adjective. Knitted with heavy hands on large needles, with huge vacuities between the strands of wool.

HEGEMONIC

adjective. Having hegemony, leadership or headship. Hegemony is very wicked, rather like Imperialism, and the word is widely employed by writers on the left to indicate any form of authority. This is the most irrelevant and silly example I could find:

> 'Refusing "the trademark of appearance ART", Hans Haack employs factual information as a basis for political and cultural critique. Below, a theoretical discussion of the sources and far-reaching implications of Haacke's challenge to HEGEMONIC methods of ART making.' (Benjamin H.D. Buchloh, writing in *ART in America*, February 1988)

Haacke 'makes' ARTWORKS of unrelentingly polemic intent. Much of it amounts to no more than journalism. For instance in 1970 he INSTALLED two transparent boxes in New York's Museum of Modern Art asking people to 'vote' in one or the other for or against Governor Rockefeller.

The excuse for this sort of saucy stunt is that he is undermining HEGEMONIC ART; threatening in some way the establishment. But his ARTWORKS do get INSTALLED in the Museum of Modern Art, and elsewhere, and no doubt command fancy prices. Who is HEGEMONIS-ING whom?

HIERARCHIC STRUCTURES

noun. A method of storing information in computers at different levels of priority.

> 'The hierarchic data structuring methods which began to appear in the early 1960s provided some relief for the entity association problem.' (*IBM Journal of Research and Development*, September 1981)

O God, those entity association blues!

HIGH-CALIBRE   *adjective*. Often the distinguishing mark of a big bore.

HIGH/LOW PROFILE   *noun*. The extent to which you are prepared to expose yourself to ridicule and abuse.

HINDUISM   *noun*. A religion whose followers demonstrate an appetite for Gods matched only by their appetite for sweetmeats. They enjoy a bewildering variety of both, and barely trouble to distinguish between them. Since such a religion has great appeal, Hindus are very numerous, and sometimes very plump.

HISTORICAL   *adjective*. Actual. Real. How it was, or is.

'The accounts have been prepared under the HISTORICAL cost convention as modified by the revaluation of certain fixed assets.' (1986 Annual Report of News International Ltd)

This means that the accounts have been prepared on the basis of the figures entered in the books at the time a transaction was made, with no subsequent adjustment for the increase or decrease in value of the assets involved. In this case the accountant has made an allowance for changes in the value of some fixed assets.

It is very touching that accountants should seize on the word HISTORICAL in their attempt to lend solidity to their abstract conjurings. They little know how insubstantial are the claims of HISTORY to represent TRUTH. Perhaps, since both parties are involved in an exercise in reassurance, there is some suitability in this borrowing.

HISTORIOGRAPHY

noun. If the historian wearies of research, he can resort to HISTORIOGRAPHY, or pooh-poohing other historians. Properly 'the writing of history', or 'the study of writing history', HISTORIOGRAPHY has become a very fashionable word in academe.

It seems to mean 'the comparative study of historians' and was sponsored – need you ask – by left-wing historians who were not at all interested in history, but very interested in discrediting any historian indifferent to their dull obsessions.

HISTORIOGRAPHY is closely allied to 'documentitis', an academic disease whose main symptom is the refusal to accept that any EVENT without supporting documents can possibly have happened. In extreme cases the patient will believe in no EVENT that cannot be illustrated from PRIMARY SOURCES, which, for some besotted reason, are held in the mind of the sufferer to be automatically more reliable, accurate and important than any other source.

HISTORY

noun. An accumulation of half-truths and evasions compiled for the benefit of academics who like to rearrange them in pretty patterns.

HISTORY is irresistibly attractive to the modern mind. It combines the authority of TRUTH wih none of the tedious disciplines necessary to establish the TRUTH. Good historians can indeed make an attempt to weigh all the available evidence in an attempt to approach the TRUTH, but that is very boring and unexciting, and they are rightly confined to the obscurity of university common rooms.

No. HISTORY belongs to the disaffected. The novelist without inspiration, the playwright without a plot, the film-maker with an axe to grind. All these can riot in the luxury that dead men can't answer back. And, since mankind shows even less originality in folly than in anything else, HISTORICAL themes are easily adapted to the current party line. (See CINEMA VERITÉ.)

HOMEOPATHY; NATUROPATHY etc.

nouns. The appearance of a prefix ending in 'O' welded directly onto the suffix 'pathy' is a sure sign that you are in the parish of the witch doctor, but you should not necessarily dismiss 'alternative medicine'. It follows the essential rule of all medicine − conventional or otherwise − that treatment must be disgusting, alarming, or both.

HOMOPHOBIA

noun. An aversion to men who do not share it.

'The new pariahs of the HOMOPHO-BIC Church of England.' (A headline on the letters page of the *Guardian*, 5.1.88)

The pariahs are the homosexual clergy, and the HOMOPHOBIA consisted of some very mild remarks by the Bishop of Rippon about the undesirability of ordaining practising homosexuals.

HOMOPHOBIA is a ridiculous modern confusion. 'Homosexual' itself is an irregular formation based on the Greek *homos*, meaning 'the same',and the Latin *sexus* meaning 'sex'. It means 'having a predilection for the same sex', or, corruptly, one with such a predilection. HOMOPHOBIA, deriving from *homos* and *phobos* (fear) should mean 'an aversion to the same', presumably, in this case, the same sex. But it is used to mean 'having an aversion to homosexuals', which is plainly not the same thing.

The root of the problem lies in 'homo'. The easy transference of 'homo' from 'homosexual' to 'HOMOPHOBIA' was made by those who thought it to come from the Latin *homo* (man). Indeed, while the mispronunciation of 'homosexual' with a long 'O' is rapidly disappearing, HOMOPHOBIA still regularly gets the long 'O' treatment. And, even if the 'homo' in HOMOPHOBIA is claimed to come independently from the Latin *homo*, 'an aversion to men' is quite as wide of the modern meaning as 'an aversion to the same sex'.

The long 'O' used to be a widespread misapprehension, but lesbians performed an uncharacteristic service to the clarity of language by insisting that they, too, were homosexuals, and the confusion was gradually cleared up. But too late to abort the delivery of HOMOPHOBIA, which is alive and well and squalling lustily.

Since the Church is so heavily engaged in these matters, let us have a resounding clerical alternative to HOMOPHOBIA. How about 'Antisodomitarianism'?

HUMAN RESOURCES *noun.* Staff. Employees. (See also PERSONNEL.) The term HUMAN RESOURCES is used by CARING managements to show that they appreciate their employees. They're not just people – they're a RESOURCE, the same as something really valuable, like coal, or iron, or bauxite. HUMAN RESOURCES are usually employees in middle or upper management. They are similar to other RESOURCES in that they are expensive, and it hurts to lose them to a competitor. HUMAN RESOURCES are at present distinct, therefore, from manpower – but not for long. CARE will filter inexorably down to the rock face, and soon every handyman/loo abluter will be that prized commodity – a HUMAN RESOURCE.

The term is both pretentious and misleading. At first sight HUMAN RESOURCES suggests 'resources that human beings have', not 'human beings who are resources'. The whole difficulty could easily be avoided by calling them staff, workers, employees, the workforce, or just 'them'.

'Effective management of HUMAN RESOURCES calls for the matching of skills requirements to corporate objectives and the establishment of formal programmes of appraisal, development, and succession planning. Also required are suitable compensation, benefit and organisation structures.' (An advertisement for AGB HUMAN RESOURCE Consultants in *Finance, the new magazine for Corporate Decision Makers,* Winter, 1987)

This is a very fruity piece of management-ese, redolent of the CREATIVE meeting where the wording of AGB's advertisement was thrashed out. It means: 'To manage staff efficiently you must make sure that each is doing a job to which he is fitted. You must also keep an eye on how they are getting on, make sure that they progress, and always have someone suitable in mind to take over whatever vacancies occur. You should offer generous insurance and pension schemes, and good salaries.'

HUMAN RIGHTS

noun. Quite different from RIGHTS, HUMAN RIGHTS are everything that a hostile state fails to provide for its subjects. This enables any state to become morally indignant at the expense of any other state, to the unspeakable benefit of international concord and understanding. (See RIGHTS.)

HURT

adjective. Damaged.

'*Better Together: Christian Partnership in a HURT City.*' (The title of a book about Liverpool by David Sheppard and Derek Worlock, respectively the Anglican Bishop and Catholic Archbishop of Liverpool)

HURT is normally applied to animate rather than inanimate objects. A case can be made for using it in the sense adopted by this brace of battling bishops, but it has the authentic soapy ring of modern nonsense, so in it goes.

It also seems an inadequate word to summarise the damage that has been done to Liverpool by modern PLANNING and ARCHITECTURE, but since Archbishop Worlock's cathedral is the *pièce de resistance* of modernism in Liverpool, no doubt he does not want to labour the point.

HYPERACTIVITY

noun. The high spirits of a child whose mother has certifiably unhinged views on child care and allows her offspring to get away with all the forms of mayhem and disorder dear to the ill-disciplined brat.

I

IDEOLOGICAL WORK GROUPS   *noun.* Thought police; possibly in some way akin to CADRES. In 1987 the Tibetan BUDDHISTS displayed their resentment of Chinese rule by rioting. The Chinese therefore installed IDEOLOGICAL WORK GROUPS in each monastery (reported in the BBC4 religious affairs programme, *Sunday*, 6.3.88) to make sure that any monk displaying less than the required solidarity with the Production Brigades should submit himself to the correct form of SELF CRITICISM.

The IDEOLOGICAL WORK GROUPS succeeded beyond their wildest dreams, and by March 1988 the Tibetans were so purged of reactionary error that they were to be seen delapidating their own monasteries, and laughingly throwing down the stones to members of the Chinese security forces in the streets below.

IDEOLOGUE   *noun.* A visionary whose visions are of very, very simple images, and whose utterances are slogans.

IDEOLOGY   *noun.* A system of ideas based on very, very simple images and slogans.

INCOMPATIBLE   *adjective.* In computers, unable to plug into each other. In marriage, unwilling to plug into each other.

IN DEPTH   *adjective.* The degree to which all modern studies are mastered. A term which disguises its own relativity. To study a pond IN DEPTH would require less effort than to study the Marianas Trench.

INDEX-LINKED — *adjective.* Inexorably bound to the roulette wheel of currency inflation.

INDIRECT RACISM — *noun.* Any attempt to avoid racial prejudice not in line with the teachings of the race relations industry.

> 'INDIRECT RACISM. A "colour blind" approach in voluntary organisations can be an indirect form of RACISM, according to *RACISM in Britain.*' (A notice in *New Society*, 12.2.88., of the book *RACISM in Britain*)

In other words, if you attempt to ignore skin colour completely you will fail in your duty to instigate POSITIVE DISCRIMINATION. RACISM is no longer prejudice against people of other races, but any failure uncritically to support the claims of groups favoured in the columns of magazines like *New Society*.

INDOLENCE — *noun.* An exquisite refinement of feeling that inhibits every attempt at activity.

INDUSTRIAL ACTION — *noun.* The means by which British trade unionists reduce their industrial activity from very little to none at all.

INFORMATION FLOW — *noun.* A COMMUNICATOR's equivalent of verbal diarrhoea.

INFORMATION CASCADE — *noun.* A COMMUNICATOR's equivalent of projectile vomiting.

INFORMATION TECHNOLOGY

noun. The prolonged echoes of William Caxton's last laugh.

INFRASTRUCTURE

noun. A word used by political economists to suggest a sturdy scaffold around which the state is built. In fact they refer to railways, roads, the electricity supply, sewers, and the postal service – indeed to all the most erratic and least dependable elements in the economy.

'Infra' and 'intra' are indispensable prefixes in manufacturing modern nonsense. Slap them onto the front of almost any word, and you have something which – at the very least – will make your interlocutor pause and rack his brains. Infradimensional. Intracyclical.

'The various capital funds which have been committed by local and central government authorities towards ensuring the regeneration of the transport INFRASTRUCTURE to service this location are significant.' (J. Scott Lowry, writing in *Property Now*, Summer 1987, about the Canary Wharf development in London's Docklands)

This is very nearly an object lesson in how not to write a sentence. Throughout it you can feel the writer shying away from stating the truth simply, presumably out of a need to feel that the transport arrangements for Canary Wharf are complicated and impressive. Why not: 'Both local and central government have provided large funds to improve transport in the docklands'?

IN-HOUSE

adjective. Used to describe FACILITIES that most sensible people would consign to the outhouse. IN-HOUSE design team;

IN-HOUSE accounting capability; IN-HOUSE medical unit; all mean: 'There is a designer/accountant/first-aid room on the premises.'

INLAND REVENUE DEPARTMENT

noun. A gang of desperados – in other respects similar to the Wild Bunch – so unlovely of aspect that not even the film industry has attempted to glamorise them.

INNER CITY

noun. Any suburb in a condition of decay. In particular any suburb whose inhabitants give way to their high animal spirits and riot. They are forced to riot by the decayed nature of their surroundings. If they can manage to hack a policeman to death as well, then it is clear that the area is so badly decayed that PLANNERS must move in and begin the work of 're-development' – a process that will force the rioters out to some other decayed area.

INNER CITY decay is held in constant equilibrium with GENTRIFICATION. They sway to and fro across the suburban townscape, one following the other, until there is every hope that in due course INNER CITY decay will be called de-GENTRIFICATION.

Very few city centres are INNER CITIES. Their decadence takes an entirely different form, and attracts almost no CARE, CONCERN, or compassion. (See URBAN PRIORITY AREAS.)

INNOVATIVE

adjective. Used of one who misrepresents old ideas so badly that they appear to be new.

INNOVATIVE is also used of things.

'This INNOVATIVE new resealing system ...' (Copy on the container of the Vacu-Vin Wine Saver, supplied by

Design Marketing Ltd, London House, Andover, Hants)

INNOVATIVE means 'having the character of innovating'. And what does 'to innovate' mean? To introduce something new, like a pump that removes the air from partly used wine bottles. 'New' was the word the Vacu-Vin manufacturer needed, and he got it, but in a fit of enthusiasm for his pump he tacked on INNOVATIVE as well. Had he thought a moment longer, he would almost certainly have decided that his pump represented the STATE OF THE ART.

INPUT *noun.* What you do to a computer – but don't get caught.

From computers INPUT has spread to embrace any sort of contribution made to anything by anyone. This is a pity, because there is a bizarre beauty in computerese, and it seems better to keep this beauty intact and unadulterated. Here surely is an example of the poetry of the future, accessed direct from my DATABASE but with no clear recall of where I saw it:

'The terminal ports on the Z960/21Q are handled by a DEDICATED INPUT/ output processor which effectively removes the onerous 1/0 processing overhead from the system processor and thus allows significantly higher levels of data THROUGHPUT.'

And while we're on the subject, here is another from an equally untraceable source:

'V-node ARCHITECTURE offers a wide range of file systems which can be integrated into the kernel configuration … In addition to the standard start-up procedures, the firmware monitor contained in on-board memory gives MENU-DRIVEN diagnostics and bootstrap software.'

It has the same appeal as the Tridentine Mass – never mind the meaning, feel the sound!

INSIDER DEALING *noun.* The unexceptionable tradition – similar to that by which a miner gets free coal – of a broker's getting free money.

INSIGHT *noun.* A species of revelation granted only to those who write in the superfluous pages of Sunday newspapers.

INSIGHTFUL *adjective.* Having INSIGHT, a disability no longer confined to barmy Highlanders and professional MEDIUMS (MEDIA?).

'Sir, The Times is to be applauded for its INSIGHTFUL leader …' (Letter to *The Times*. 15.2.88)

It was, of course, the *Sunday Times* which started the rot where INSIGHT is concerned by having an 'INSIGHT Team'. It was too much to hope that the rot would not spread to the leader columns of its sister paper.

All whimsical feature-page headings – INSIGHT, Focus, SPECTRUM, etc – should be mocked off the page. It is a favourite device of lazy EDITORS, desperate to fill space with anything, to devise catch-all, meaningless titles so that they may cram women's lunar difficulties cheek by jowl with goldfish maintenance.

INSTALLATION *noun.* Modern ART-talk for an exhibit.

'A similar reversal of Enlightenment ideas could be seen in Jenny Holzer's

INSTALLATION ...' (Paul Groot, 'Et in Arcadia Ego', contribution to *artscribe*, January 1988)

'Exhibit' would do just as well, but INSTALLATION has satisfying industrial undertones.

INSTANTANEOUS DISASSEMBLY

noun. An explosion. When safely removed from the public, or perpetrated by officially recognised public enemies, explosions are excellent news fodder, and should be mentioned wherever possible. When they occur under the aegis of a government department or a great corporation, they are too dramatic for public consumption. Where nuclear power stations are concerned, even the possibility of an explosion must be glossed over. When such a possibility arose at Three Mile Island, it was referred to as INSTANTANEOUS DISASSEMBLY. (See RAPID OXIDATION).

INTEGRITY CHECK

noun. A procedure regularly undertaken by computerists, whose machines notoriously lack integrity and are prone to whizz off the rails into a morass of digital turpitude.

INTELLECTUAL

noun. One who works with his head rather than with his hands – like a human cannonball.

INTERFACE

noun. 1. The zone where a dramatic CONFRONTATION takes place between two INCOMPATIBLE computers.
2. By extension of its computerese meaning, any area where systems or functions collide. The 'marine-terrestial ecozonal INTERFACE' is – to you and me – the tideline or foreshore.

'The Human Factors Engineering Group is responsible for human-engineering operator INTERFACES throughout the Sizewell plant ... ' (Advertisement in *The Times*, 14.1.88., for ERGONOMISTS and engineers to work for the Central Electricity Generating Board)

This is perhaps the most exciting INTERFACE of all, where Röntgens and Gamma rays drift about like thistledown. The opaque terminology is employed so that everyone may look at this matter through a glass darkly, rather than INTERFACE to INTERFACE. The advertisement is for engineers and scientists to think up ways of making it safer to work with radioactive material. A laudable aim, but one which must be expressed obliquely in case cynics might ask if the CEGB's procedures were not perfectly safe already.

Note how modern techniques of sentence construction effortlessly defeat any attempt to disentangle meaning from the words 'human-engineering operator INTER-FACES'. Are we dealing with an operator in human-engineering who INTERFACES with something or other? Or are we dealing with an INTERFACE between human operators and some sort of engineering? Or perhaps operators of human-engineering INTERFACE with each other? The hyphen suggests that 'human-engineering' is an adjective qualifying 'operator'. That indicates the third of these interpretations. But in spite of this evidence, I go for number two. The CONFRONTATION promises to be more dramatic.

INTERFAITH DIALOGUE   *noun.* A Holy War of words.

INTERSUBJECTIVITY *noun.* Shared subjectivity. Getting close to objectivity, but used by people to whom objectivity is anathema. The idea is that if two people share the same subjective convictions, or if two phenomena share the same subjective terms of definition, that's as close to objectivity as you're going to get. (See POST STRUCTURALISM.)

'An unbroken INTERSUBJECTIVITY of the grammar in force would certainly make possible the identity of meanings and thereby constant relations of understanding, but would simultaneously annihilate the identity of the I in communications with others.' (Jurgen Habermass, *Zur Logik der Socialwissenschaften*, Frankfurt, 1970. Quoted in *Logics of Disintegration* by Peter Dews, Verso, 1987)

The left are at pains to discount the idea of objectivity. Too many of the 'hard' sciences produce results that support conservative modes of thought and behaviour. Unthinkable. Their METHODOLOGY must be at fault. Let's develop a philosophy that denies the claim that the human mind can be objective. That'll scupper them.

Unfortunately, it means that the new philosophy can't be objective either.

One of the most marked characteristics of the human mind is its ability to get outside itself and 'think from outside' – in other words to be objective – and this characteristic has been the bane of zealots throughout history. But the fact that objectivity is only one mental characteristic displayed by mankind allows the modern zealot to insinuate the doubts of relativism.

The quoted passage seems to be saying that individual identity can be preserved only at the cost of forgoing full INTER-SUBJECTIVITY, which alone would make it possible to share fully the neutral, exact meanings of words. Poppycock. If I were to give vent to the passionately subjective cry 'All POST-STRUCTURALISTS are verbose nincompoops', the words would carry my exact meaning to the POST-STRUC-TURALISTS without our having shared one jot, tittle, or smidgeon of INTER-SUBJECTIVITY.

INTERTEXTUALITY *noun.* Plagiarism. This definition I myself plagiarised from Malcolm Bradbury, who employs it in his novella *Cuts*.

More grandly, INTERTEXTUALITY is the POST-STRUCTURALIST term for the way in which 'texts' influence each other. It is the modern critical way of expressing the obvious and dull truth that writers are literate (or used to be) and have therefore read the works of other writers, and been to some extent influenced by them.

> 'Furthermore this same structure can also be discerned in the relations between the texts, so that interpretation is impossibe without the recognition of an INTERTEXTUALITY, in which the meaning of the text is modulated by other contiguous texts, and the meaning of these in turn by further texts, in a process which has no discernible boundaries.' (Peter Dews, *The Logics of Disintegration*)

No discernible boundaries either, of course, to the Lit Crit biz whose job it is to interpret these texts.

All admirers of the modern mind must note and relish Mr Dews's mellifluous use of 'modulated' and 'contiguous'.

IRRECONCILABLE DIFFERENCES

noun. Unanimous matrimonial accord as to each other's unbearability.

ISLAM

noun. A religion that has trailed behind its main competitor, Christianity, by threatening potential converts with the awful prospect of four wives, and no liquor.

ISLAMICISM

noun. The Muslim equivalent of LIBERATION THEOLOGY. A partly understood attempt to reconcile partly understood passages of the Koran with partly understood passages from Karl Marx, Vladimir Ilyich Lenin, old Uncle Tom Cobbleigh, and all.

J

JUDAISM

noun. The most terrifying of all the great religions. The Jews worship a God who for centuries has treated them with unremitting severity, culminating in the massacre of six million of them at the hands of one of the barbarian tribes of northern Europe. In spite of this the Jews persist – against all the evidence – in the belief that Jahweh will one day deliver them. As an example of hope springing eternal in the human breast, the Jewish faith is unequalled. It should by now be plain to the meanest intelligence that Jahweh *dislikes* the Jews.

JUDICIAL ACTIVIST

noun. A member of the American Supreme Court who takes advantage of defects in the AMERICAN CONSTITUTION to amend to his liking laws passed by the Legislature.

Used freely of the 'liberal' judges of the Supreme Court, as in the radio programme *In Order to Form a More Perfect Union* (BBC Radio 3, 26.10.87).

It is the use of the word ACTIVIST that betrays the nonsense lurking within the dignified proceedings of the Supreme Court. The notion of an active judge is rather alarming, but the term indicates merely judges of a reforming turn of mind, anxious to help women slay their unborn children, and bent on compelling debussers to bus. (See ACTIVIST.)

K

KIDS

noun. The young of the DISADVAN-TAGED, very rarely singular.

The middle classes have KIDS too, but they are not so seriously AT RISK as their poorer namesakes, and scarcely deserve the designation. And although they are seldom to be found in care, the middle classes patronise a schooling system that obviates any such need. (See PUBLIC.)

L

LATERAL THINKING *noun.* Jumping sideways to conclusions.

'Vertical thinking is for using ideas and LATERAL THINKING is for changing them.'

'LATERAL THINKING is to do with changing perceptions and finding new ways of looking at things.'

'LATERAL THINKING turns creativity into a tool.'

'The CONCEPT of LATERAL THINKING was originated by the author in 1966.'

(All taken from Edward de Bono, *Word-power*, 1977)

LATERAL THINKING is as old as the human mind. It is no more than the technique of asking yourself 'What happens if I do it this way?' Dr de Bono has codified its techniques in several books, and likes to suggest that there is a collision between LATERAL THINKING and 'vertical', or logical, thinking. The inference is that LATERAL THINKING is or could be as important an intellectual system as logical thought.

Dr de Bono also likes to suggest that our thinking is dominated (to its disadvantage) by 'vertical' thinking, from which it needs to be freed by our unexploited LATERAL gifts. In fact it is the other way about. People have always been prone to fly to the extremes of their thought, to imagine

138

things, and to make unconnected associations. Logical thought evolved as a discipline to curb the volatility of the human mind, and has to be taught before our 'LATERAL', associative powers can be of any use.

LAW

noun. The system of *Purse Majeure* which replaced *Force Majeure* as civilisation grew increasingly flabby.

LDCs (LESS DEVELOPED COUNTRIES)

noun. Hinterlands begat colonies; colonies begat dependencies; dependencies begat underdeveloped nations; underdeveloped nations begat developing nations; and developing nations begat LDCs. It seems a retrograde step. But the process did not stop there because LDCs begat the Third World, and the Third World begat the South. (See DEVELOPING.)

LEADING EDGE

noun and *adjective.* In its original context of aircraft design, this was a vivid image. The meaning of 'the LEADING EDGE' or 'the trailing edge' of a wing is instantly clear, even to a layman. But the term has been hijacked by all and sundry, and is now synonymous with STATE OF THE ART.

'Since … 1969 IBM has been incorporating LEADING EDGE technology in products referred to as small general purpose systems.' (*IBM Journal of Research and Development,* September, 1981)

Why 'referred to'? Are they not small, general purpose systems? If not, what are they, and why are they 'referred to' by a misleading term? The whole sentence should read: 'Since 1969 IBM has been incorporating new techniques in its range of small, general-purpose products'.

LEARNING CURVE *noun.* A borrowing from the exciting world of graphs, your LEARNING CURVE is the measure of your capacity to master brain-bogglingly dull subjects. To have a long or shallow LEARNING CURVE is the sign of a civilised and fastidious mind. Steep or fast learners are bores and swots.

Alternatively, LEARNING CURVE is a measure of time. 'I'm well into the LEARNING CURVE,' a trainee computerist might brag.

There is a touching optimism in this usage. It assumes that learning gets easier as it goes on – hence the falling-off in the steepness of the curve. Once you've passed a certain point on the parabola, it's all downhill.

A likely tale.

It is more probable that people on a LEARNING CURVE have a very short ATTENTION SPAN, and that after this period has elapsed they are simply not learning at all. They may be said to have gone clean round the curve.

'We're in a kind of LEARNING CURVE situation ...' (Sir Roy Strong, interviewed on the BBC radio programme *Kaleidoscope*, 28.12.87, speaking of the disappointing public response to the opening of the Theatre Museum)

Surely, where going clean round the curve is concerned, once a Knight is enough?

LEGACY-OF-COLONIALISM *noun.* The lawlessness that prevails after the restraints of colonialism have been removed. (See DEVELOPING.)

LEGITIMATE DEMANDS *noun.* Demanding money with menaces.

LEVERAGED MANAGEMENT BUY OUT *noun.* Not far removed from a sell out. The *coup d'état* of commerce which, like its political equivalent, is financed by interested parties.

LIBERALISM *noun.* The political doctrine that the moral comfort of the holder comes before all other considerations. So long as the liberal conscience is clear, all is well. But the liberal conscience requires frequent stoking with the backslidings of political systems to the right of LIBERALISM, and would quickly burn itself out without the iniquities of conservatives, monarchists, dictators, military officers, fox-hunters and Boers to keep it going.

For some reason the malefactions of regimes to the left of LIBERALISM are of no help in stoking the fires of conscience, and they are largely ignored. Whole peoples may be forcibly transported, freedom extinguished, Jews picked on, forced labour practised on a vast scale – and so long as these things are done to the right background music of hideous revolutionary jargon, the liberal conscience remains unmoved. It is, indeed, a beast easily placated by hideous jargon.

A liberal conscience is not, of course, the exclusive property of paid-up members of the Liberal Party. It is rife among the wetter sort of Socialist, especially in the higher ranks of the Church of England. It is above all an expression of self-importance. 'The comfort of my lofty conscience stands above all. I don't care how unreal its manifestations are. I don't care how dreadful its consequences may be. All that matters is that I should *feel* right, and be seen to *be* right.'

And by one of those merciful dispensations that nearly persuades one there must be a God after all, the consequences are never dreadful for the Liberal's standard of living, which is high, and often indirectly supported by various conservative, authoritarian, military, and even racialist regimes here and there about the globe.

If you think I exaggerate, rivet your attention on the Liberal administration of 1906-1910. It passed the Trades Disputes Act and the South Africa Act. Overwhelmed with compassion for the working classes, the Liberals actually granted trade unions immunity from the consequences of their actions at civil law, a disaster which forced the British electorate to the desperate lengths – 73 years later – of summoning up Mrs Thatcher to redress the balance. In South Africa they gave the whole caboodle back to the Boers, simply because Lord Kitchener had been so beastly to them. In the wake of these two monumental howlers LIBERALISM was in tremendous trim, aglow with merit.

LIBERATION THEOLOGY

noun. An AFFIRMATIVE philosophy adopted by the Christian churches to ensure the enslavement of as many people as possible to secular, totalitarian regimes.

LIBERTARIAN

noun. Not, as you may think, one devoted to liberty, but an intolerant authoritarian, not far removed from a fascist.

' ... a determined push by the right, some of whom have close links with

LIBERTARIAN extremists, to over-throw 30 years of centre-left control of the Young Conservatives.' (A report by Nicholas Wood and Sheila Gunn on the Young Conservatives, in *The Times*, 15.2.88)

In other words, these LIBERTARIANS are still further to the right than the would-be Putsch-ites in the Young Conservatives. If they are truly LIBERTARIANS, then we have nothing to fear from CONSERVATIVES, but this is not the inference that the report intends.

I have no doubt that Wood and Gunn were following the highest traditions of impartial reporting, and it is very illuminating that they should use the word LIBERTARIAN in this context, coupled with 'extremist'. It is also a well-developed piece of modern nonsense.

The perjorative echoes that now resound from LIBERTARIAN are clearly audible in the quoted passage, and they demonstrate how LIBERTARIAN has swung through 180° in the minds of the intelligentsia, from approval to disapproval. How has this come about?

It originates in the fact that left-wing governments – even of the mild sort experienced in Britain under the Labour Party – make so free with the individual's RIGHTS, that their opponents are able to parade under the banner of individual liberty. And so, in the eyes of the left, a LIBERTARIAN is now a heartless, besuited yahoo, who does not care about pensioners, GAYS, BLACKS, the National Health Service, free milk, or any of the other great SOCIALIST causes. (See SELF-STYLED).

But the fact that the left can use

LIBERTARIAN as a pejorative, and have not bothered to invent some other unflattering term, tells us what they think of liberty.

LIFE-DAMAGING CONDITIONS

noun. Deformity or handicap in the unborn child. This is a term used by the pro-abortion lobby to soften the harsh fact that they recommend killing deformed babies. Once out of the womb the 'handicapped kid' is the target of intense sentiment on the part of the CARING and CONCERNED. In the womb it seems easier to get rid of them. But if you suggest that you are merely relieving a LIFE-DAMAGING CONDITION, it sounds better than killing deformed children.

'Not all LIFE-DAMAGING CONDITIONS can be detected by doctors before 18 weeks.' (Leader in *The Times*, 22.1.88, dealing with the proposed reduction of the legal time limit on abortions from 28 to 18 weeks)

There is a perfectly good alternative to abortion which, so far as I know, no-one but myself has yet put forward. In the case of all unwanted pregnancies – kill the father.

'LIFE-DAMAGING CONDITIONS' is a beautifully-modulated piece of modern humbug. The spurious concern. The reverentially hushed tone. The vagueness of the word CONDITION. The curious idea of DAMAGING LIFE, particularly when presented as being worse than taking life.

Sometimes the variant 'Life Threatening Conditions' crops up, both in this context, and in the bizarre deliberations of those who try to codify the behaviour of animals. A typical sentence might be 'Flight-response behaviour varies exponentially to the intensity of life-threatening conditions.' In other words, 'the more frightened they are, the faster they run.'

LIVING WAGE

noun. A notional RIGHT promised by trade union leaders to their members. An imaginary emolument, index-linked to the price of television sets and video recorders.

LOMI LETTER (OF MORAL INTENT)

noun. A document in which a member of the business community expresses a general intention to do something without incurring any concrete obligation. The correct definition is given in the *Macmillan Dictionary of International Finance*:

> 'An undertaking by a company which falls short of a legal guarantee.' (Julia Walmsley, *Macmillan Dictionary of International Finance*)

One can always rely on the business community to put morality firmly in its place – well downstream of legal guarantees.

LOSS ADJUSTER

noun. An expert in small print, who can find sizes even tinier than those already deployed by your insurance company.

'LOSS ADJUSTER' is a very beautiful and subtle euphemism. There is no indication of whose loss is being adjusted. At first glance it might even be yours, but it is, of course, your insurance company's. And in what way is it being adjusted? It is, of course, being reduced. The LOSS ADJUSTER is employed by your insurance company to find excuses for reducing your claim. It is honest and revealing of your insurance company to refer to your claim – which you have insured with many heavy premiums – as a LOSS. It is less straightforward to refer to their heavies as ADJUSTERS.

LOVE

noun. 1. A sensation imparted to the male heart by contemplating the female figure. A sensation imparted to the female *abdomina* by contemplating male balance figures.

2. The desperate calculation – half hope and half despair – that one *could* do worse and might very well *not* do better.

LOW OBSERVABLE

adjective. Difficult to see. Used of an American bombing aircraft designed to baffle the USSR's radar defences.

Doubling-up the adjectives LOW and OBSERVABLE creates a confusion, because the two words are not properly related to each other. Is the aircraft more OBSERVABLE when it's LOW? Or is its observability of a low order? The USAF intend the second meaning, but with nothing other than LOW OBSERVABLE to go by, it might more probably be the first.

The Pentagon is usually quicker on the draw with the floppy phrase. The point is that the aircraft is not entirely undetectable by radar. So 'Radar Proof' would be out. But how about 'Radar Negative'; or 'Radar Insensitive'? (See SENSITIVE.)

However, there is another term for this aircraft which demonstrates how much superior idiom is to technical jargon. It is also called the 'Stealth' bomber. Neither term is strictly accurate about the capabilities of the 'plane, but the idiomatic term gives a far clearer idea of how it is intended to sneak up on Minsk and wipe it off the map.

LYRIC

noun. Words intended to be sung to the accompaniment of a lyre. Hence the name of a despicably primitive school of poetry patronised by Pindar, Homer, Sophocles and other like defectives. Mercifully the inexorable march of progress has raised the LYRIC above its embarrassing origins, and it now characterises the wordless grunts and yells by which popular musicians express their rutting tendencies.

M

MAISONETTE

noun. A vertical flat.

Some MAISONETTES, however, go sideways as well as up and down.

'One of the largest MAISONETTES in Eaton Square, constructed laterally across two buildings and having 12 windows overlooking the private gardens. The MAISONETTE was carefully designed and fitted using the finest quality craftsmen ... £2,300,000.' (Advertisement by Aylesford in *Country Life*, 19.11.87)

That's £191,666 per window, and goodness knows how much per Finest Quality Craftsman, with whom the MAISONETTE seems to be crammed. Surely if you are soliciting two and a quarter million pounds of someone else's money you should be able to find someone to write your advertisement in English, and also to find a more dignified term than twee nonsense like MAISONETTE.

One is prey to the suspicion that the price has influenced the description. If this property is arranged laterally, surely it is a flat? There is no size restriction on a flat. Even the idea that a flat is all on one floor has been eroded. Why is this property a MAISONETTE? Only because it seems a bit steep to ask £2,300,000 for a mere flat.

MANAGED NEWS

noun. Mismanaged fiction. MANAGED NEWS, like DISINFORMATION, is misleading government information. MAN-

AGED NEWS is usually for the consumption of the press and broadcasters, while DISINFORMATION is fed to other governments (sometimes, of course, through the press).

News management has become a major technique in the art of government, but it has one insuperable disadvantage. Among all the lies issuing daily from the fertile pens of journalists, the lies of government go largely unnoticed.

MARINE HABITAT

noun. Submerged scrap metal.

'The Greenpeace vessel Rainbow Warrior leaving harbour yesterday to be sunk as a MARINE HABITAT off New Zealand.' (Caption in *The Times*, 2.12.87)

Greenpeace is a worthy organisation, much persecuted by the Deuxième Bureau and other enemies of the ENVIRONMENT, but there is something po-faced about grabbing these extra brownie marks by committing the *Rainbow Warrior* to everlasting environmental service. The ship's environmental function, once submerged, would be the same regardless of who sunk her or why. Were the wicked French creating a MARINE HABITAT when they sent her to the bottom? No. They were just making a frightful mess in Auckland harbour. There is also a contrast between the Arcadian associations normal to the word HABITAT, and the leaky, oily, rusty old tub being towed out to become a glorified lobster pot.

A passing thought, however, for those tremendous HABITAT enhancers, the Kriegsmarine.

MARKET LEADERSHIP *noun*. Cornering so much of the market that your competitors are dissuaded from following you into it.

MARKET MAKERS *noun*. Modern nonsense for Jobbers and Brokers. Dealers in stocks and shares used to be known as Brokers (those acting on a customer's behalf), and Jobbers (those holding stocks and shares on their own account and quoting buying and selling prices for them)

As these rôles merged in the wake of BIG BANG, however, the old terms were felt to be pejorative. They smacked of trade. The yearning for CREATIVE endeavour made itself felt among the fresh young graduates in the money business. 'What do we *make*?' they asked themselves, in agonies of introspection. Of course they make nothing, but by quoting the prices of their holdings they influence other stockholders, and the sum of these grasping activities is a market in stocks. They therefore gave themselves the bold, merchant-venturing name MARKET MAKERS.

MARKETPLACE *noun*. Just as Christendom is the sum of all Christians, and the Umma of all Muslims, so the MARKETPLACE is the sum of all CONSUMERS, and the object of almost equal devotional piety.

As an abstraction the MARKETPLACE obsesses economists in the same way that the GRASS ROOTS obsess politicians, and the battle-zone generals. It is where it all happens, but they can never be quite sure what.

'If you're active in the international MARKETPLACE, you need a professional service organization with world-wide resources.' (*Proven Professionals*, a brochure advertising the services of Touche Ross, a 'BROAD BASED Professional Services Firm')

'If you trade abroad' would surely be more straightforward.

MARXISM TODAY

proper noun. Stalinism yesterday, and Leninism the day before that.

MARXIST

noun. The clever elder brother of the Fascist family who got to university. MARXIST-LENINIST: *noun.* the clever elder brother in later life, having contracted a disastrous *mésalliance* to acquire great estates, and, like many another to marry property, having hyphenated his name in the process.

MEANINGFUL

adjective. Meaningless.

'It is a MEANINGFUL reminder in a context where it really matters ... It is a very competitive society, a very conservative society, one in which women are liable to be discriminated against in one way or another. It may be subtle.' (Wayne Godley, Professor of Applied Economics at Cambridge University, reported in the *Independent*, 31.10.88, on the decision to rewrite the University's statutes in 'gender-free' terms [see EQUAL OPPORTUNITIES])

You do not apply economics through the medium of the English tongue, apparently, otherwise Professor Godley would be aware that he has labelled his competitive and conservative society 'subtle' as well. I think his meaning is that the means of discrimination against women may be subtle.

His 'meaningful reminder' is the expenditure of quite large funds to go through the University's Statutes picking up every instance of the pronoun 'he' being used to 'subsume the female gender'.

It is an exercise that should be applied to all literature, including the Psalms.

'What is person, that thou art mindful of him/her?'

MEDIA BIAS

noun. The bone-headed refusal of journalists to toe your party line.

> 'Fourthly, for the Labour leadership to launch a meaningful campaign for MEDIA reform would be to bring down the wrath of the press and television. The concept that the MEDIA should never be touched by state intervention has a very powerful cultural and historical hold.' (Denis MacShane in *Tribune*, 8.1.88)

He goes on to call for 'incremental, implementable reform'. (He probably congratulated himself for bringing off this association of sounds.) Earlier in the same passage, he bewails the 'Tory-YUPPIE-takeover of the BBC', and the unmistakable tenor of his article is that the BBC *should* be subject to state intervention, so long as his gang is running the state. Tory 'YUPPIES' having a say in the affairs of the corporation is out, but Tribunites and their friends 'implementing incremental reforms' is OK.

Equally damning examples of unconscious candour could no doubt be found on the Tory side. I am loth to say anything that might aid or comfort the BBC, but while both main political parties continue to yelp about MEDIA BIAS, it can't all be wrong.

MEDIUM

noun. A person through whom spirits speak. MEDIA: *plur. noun.* A collection of people through whom spirits speak. And wines. And beers.

MEGO

exclamation. the acronym of 'My Eyes Glaze Over'. A humorous but silly expression of stupefied disbelief. Asked to contemplate something truly unimaginable – the size of the universe, or a tax rebate of £13.47p. – one might throw up one's hands and say 'MEGO!'.

MENU-DRIVEN

adjective. Determined by the computer program you have selected.

'The 40-character display talks to you in a friendly, MENU-DRIVEN DIA-LOGUE, so that anyone in your organisation can walk up and use the Xerox 7020 straight away.' (Brochure explaining the Rank Xerox 7020 copying machine)

A MENU-DRIVEN DIALOGUE sounds like a blazing row with the head waiter.

METHODOLOGY

noun. A word which deceitfully suggests method, thinks better of it, and candidly degenerates into an onomatopoeic mess of discombobulated 'ology' which accurately reflects the state of mind of a methodologist.

'The METHODOLOGY Rogers uses for creation of this space is to separate short-life and long-life elements.' (Jane Robins, talking to Richard Rogers, designer of the Centre Pompidou, Paris, and the Lloyd's Building, London. *Square Mile*, 1984)

To be able to distinguish between what will last and what will not last scarcely seems to merit a word as weighty as METHODOLOGY.

MICROWAVE

noun. Raw food, though nourishing, is often unpalatable. Cooking is the process of making it palatable. The MICROWAVE takes us one step further. Food already cooked is frozen, to preserve it for a later day. When required it is placed in the MICROWAVE whose action jiggles the molecular components of the food in such a way that it is rendered even less palatable than it was to start with. In cooking unfrozen food from scratch the MICRO-WAVE produces much the same result. Such are the wonders of science.

The MICROWAVE is the measure of the sloth, incompetence, and barbarous nature of modern man – or should it be woman? Cooking food is fundamental to human living. It is one of the great civilised arts. It should be a delight to spend time, trouble and ingenuity in preparing a meal. But modern man prefers to go to the freezer, get out a solid lump, and in three of four positron-pulverising minutes reduce it to a soggy mass. He and she deserve all the ailments that accrue from these slovenly and unhealthy habits, including, I hope, hitherto unsuspected long-term effects of MICROWAVE cooking.

MIDDLE AGE

noun. The time of life when hangovers begin to last for two or more days.

MIDDLE AGES

noun. The centuries-long hangover of Pontius Pilate's lax methods of admin-istration.

MILITANT

noun. One who will fight on behalf of the workers to the last drop of the workers' blood.

MINIMALISM

noun. The prevalence of minimal talent, minimal intellect and minimal technique in the modern arts.

MEGAFORMS

noun. Very large animals like mammoths and giant sloths.

> 'The MEGAFORMAL Extinction process ... '(Dr Peter Moore, *Science Now*, BBC Radio 4, 25.1.88)

Some eleven thousand years ago all the mammoths suddenly turned up their toes. Until recently this was blamed on the climate, but along comes Dr Moore and says it was the result of a lot of stone age Calibans clouting the creatures with clubs. Man was to blame. Personally I believe that they, the mammoths, witnessed in horror the conduct of man, realised in due course they would be called MEGAFORMS, and died of despair.

MODERN MUSIC

noun. A sequence of silences made unbearable by the knowledge of what will succeed them.

MODULE

noun. Closely related to a UNIT, but none can say how. MODULE has always presented difficulties, and even the *OED* admits confusion over its original meaning. The clearest and most precise meaning it has enjoyed over the years is, in the classical 'orders', the UNIT of length by which the proportions of the other parts are measured.

Here is a modern use of MODULE, which in spite of being drawn from the world of architecture, does not seem to refer to the classical orders.

> 'The uniformity of the innumerable windows in this vast wall on the Piazza

San Marco gives the same play as would the smooth sides of a room ... The pigeons of St Mark's themselves add their own uniform MODULE, providing a varied and effective note in the scheme.' (Le Corbusier, *The City of Tomorrow*, 1924)

It could almost be a song. 'Pigeon MODULES keep falling on my head.'

MODULE now seems to mean 'a standard UNIT of production.'

MORALITY   *noun*. Simultaneously the cloak *and* dagger of the will.

MOREISH   *adjective*. Wine-blurbese for 'stimulating the appetite for more'.

'Heather and honey, rich, weighty, very clean, very subtle, very MOREISH.' (Charles Sydney, commenting on a Madeira in *Wine*, New Year 1988)

Almost any alcohol that is not actually toxic stimulates the appetite for more. Perhaps the insinuation is that hardened tasters are indifferent to the vulgar pleasures of boozing, and that to make *them* want more it *must* be good.

MORTGAGE TAX RELIEF   *noun*. An immense bribe, offered by governments of a conservative tendency, to lure a loth and leaden-footed electorate into the middle class.

MOTIVATED   *adjective*. Sufficiently witless to give an impression of enthusiasm for one's work.

'Our modern purpose-built offices provide a lively and competitive environment for enthusiastic, self- MOTIVATED people for whom sales achievements are a priority.' (Advertisement in *The Times*, 14.1.88, for Advertisement Sales EXECUTIVES for News Group Newspapers)

I suppose it is asking too much that such a rarified beast as an Advertisement Sales EXECUTIVE could exist outside an 'ENVIRONMENT'. Is it the 'ENVIRONMENT' itself which is lively and competitive, or the other self-MOTIVATED EXECUTIVES who share the ENVIRONMENT? 'People for whom sales achievements are a priority' are, presumably, merely people who like selling things.

MOULD-BREAKING   *adjective.* The deep illiterate confusions of the modern mind have associated MOULD-BREAKING with 'pathfinding', or disrupting some established pattern. The British SDP Party was said to have BROKEN THE MOULD of British politics. In other words, it had added a fourth party to the three traditional parties. It had disrupted the established pattern.

Moulds were broken, of course, to preserve the rarity of the artefacts cast in them. 'They BROKE THE MOULD when they made the likes of him' is a salute to someone's singularity, similar to saying 'They don't make them like that any more'. To BREAK A MOULD is not to initiate a new venture but to prevent imitation, proliferation and debasement.

No one with a clear picture of what a mould is, and what the consequences of breaking it are, could possibly use MOULD-BREAKING in its modern sense. It is not the fault of the victims of COMPREHENSIVE EDUCATION that they have no clear picture of anything in their heads, but they should be discouraged from working on newspapers where their mistaken coinages can gain popular currency.

MS

noun. The title and style of a woman who feels disqualified for one reason or another, from Lady, Mrs or Miss.

We can leave 'Lady' aside. Mrs is exclusive to married women – in spite of being a contraction of Mistress – and Miss seems to cover the rest of the field, being applied both to spinsters and young girls. How has the hideous, vowelless monosyllable MS crept in?

The answer is not feminist zeal, but laziness in letter writing. Rather than find out whether one's correspondent is married or not, it is easier just to put the slovenly MS on the envelope.

But having gained currency through convenience, MS finds itself at the centre of the battle of the sexes. Feminists have decided that it is neutral, lacking any suggestion of condescension or servile status. As a result it is rapidly assuming the spinsterish associations that once belonged to Miss.

MYTHOS

noun. General cultural background. Body of myths. Cultural ambience. A lazy avoidance of having to analyse in greater detail the 'general cultural background' of whatever is being discussed. Often used in a disparaging sense, as though myths constituted the greater part of the said cultural background.

'Although the neo-expressionism of Clemente and others has done little to advance critical DISCOURSE, here the MYTHOS with which the artist surrounds himself at least inspires some virtuoso paint handling.' (John Miller, 'Stations', a contribution to *artscribe*, January 1988)

Paint handling is, of course, Modern Nonsense for 'brushwork'. But brushwork is no longer quite accurate because modern artists are not happy unless they can use hands, feet, rollers, bicycles, even naked girls, and many other methods of applying paint.

A very daring reading of this passage allows one to conclude that the MYTHOS in question is neo-expressionism. What may come as a surprise is that 'to advance critical DISCOURSE' is the purpose of the artist.

N

NATURISM

noun. A 'movement' – like pacifism or SOCIALISM – and like them equipped with a special language, Nudespeak. But NATURISM is not nudism. O no.

'NATURISM was defined some years ago ... as "nudism which socialises itself".' (Phil Vallack, writing in *Clothing-Optional Life*, an American NATURIST magazine, 1987)

Like any good movement, NATURISM is divided against itself. Club NATURISTS vie with Beach NATURISTS. The outdoor set constantly lament the restrictions on their freedom. No sooner do they find an isolated river bank than mobs of anglers turn up. I see their point. A set of size 8 treble hooks whizzing through the air is enough to bring on a very sharp attack of BODY-GUILT, not to say 'clothes-compulsion'.

Any temptation to deride NATURISM is immediately offset by dumbstruck amazement at some of the places where NATURISTS choose to naturise. Here are a few.

Chatteringhaws Loch.
Horncliffe-on-Tweed.
Northwest of Kinbrace.
Loch Maree.
Glen Ogle.
Lancaster Canal.

It is superfluous for me to add that there is a Cardigan NATURIST Group.

NECKTIE (American), TIE (English)   *noun.* An article of apparel, given by women to men on whom they have designs, representing a flag of possession, a phallic symbol, and a hangman's noose.

NEEDS   *noun.* the luxuries you pay for with other people's money.

NEEDS-ORIENTATED   *adjective.* Somewhere between PRODUCT-dominated and customer-led. I think.

NEGATIVE   *adjective.* Positive that someone else's enthusiasm is misplaced.

NEGOTIATION   *noun.* The insistence on Draconian conditions backed up by the threat of INDUSTRIAL ACTION or other forms of disguised violence if they are not met.

NEO-COLONIALISM   *noun.* Making more money out of a backward country than its indigenous masters are able to do.

NEO-DARWINISM   *noun.* A grotesque masquerade intended to illumine the origins of life, in which the ghost of Charles Darwin appears draped in the monkish habit of Gregor Mendel.

NEWSWORTHY   *adjective.* Measuring down to the lowest notch on the yardstick of infamy.

NOBEL PRIZES   *noun.* Annual sacrifices made amid much incense-burning and many incantations to appease the unquiet shade of a Swedish explosives manufacturer.

It is very creditable that the Swedes have managed to produce both an armaments millionaire and enough representatives of the modern elect to form a panel of judges for his prizes. It is, after all, a small country, plunged in sub-arctic gloom for half the year.

However, although I am all for tormenting the good, it is cruel to expect elderly members of the intelligentsia to form up in the bitter cold of a Stockholm November to be harangued in a tongue none of them understands.

Could not Mr Nobel's guilty conscience be appeased in some other way? Milk-white virgins perhaps – if any can be found?

NON-VIOLENCE *noun*. The pacifism of those who have delegated the need to commit violent deeds to others. In a sense all pacifists do this, since no pacifist could exist outside a society prepared to use force to defend his right to be a pacifist. But here is a pacifist with a difference.

> 'We will shake them and we will drive them out of our midst, and if they are not careful they might find that they run risks in what they do – one of which may be having their skulls cracked – as none of us can predict what form the anger they raise takes, however much I may be personally committed to NON-VIOLENCE.' (A speech attributed in the *Spectator* (October 1987) to Nkosi Dr Mengosuthu Buthelezi, chief minister of Zululand, or Kwazulu in modern nonsense)

The notion of a NON-VIOLENT Zulu is new to me, and revolutionary. What is a Zulu *for*, if not blithely and bloodily to ply knobkerrie and assegai?

The greatest mistake ever made by the British Empire was to incorporate Zululand into Natal, and thence into the Union of South Africa. It should have been maintained as an independent kingdom, and its surplus manpower recruited into British regiments, like the Ghurkas.

Then the surprised Germans could have tasted the fruits of NON-VIOLENCE.

NORMAL READING AGE

noun. A measure of literacy, arranged so that at any stage of development the average child shows no sign that he or she might in due course read better than the teacher. As a result of this wise provision the vast majority of British schoolchildren are of above NORMAL READING AGE.

NOUNS as VERBS

Much modern nonsense is concocted not by inventing unnecessary words, but by incurable and deplorable fancies of syntax. One of these is using nouns as verbs.

'We are especially focusing on those women who may SELF-HARM as a way of expressing this distress.' (Diane Harrison, in a letter to *Spare Rib* January 1988)

'Do themselves harm'? 'Damage themselves'? 'Hurt themselves'?

NOUVELLE CUISINE

noun. The ART of charging more money for less food.

NUCLEAR FREE

adjective. Exempt from the effects of Soviet nuclear attack by decree of the all-powerful environmental sub-committee of your local council.

NUDESWIM

noun. Nudespeak for skinny dipping. To

NATURISTS the whole thing is a ritual of almost processional solemnity.

'Nudeswim and sauna sessions only ...'

'Parson's Pleasure, traditional semi-sacred NUDESWIM for clothesless academics ...'

'At Merryfields some enthusiasts welcome the New Year by NUDESWIM in the pool.' (All taken from *Inland Free Sun*, 1988)

NUDEWALK (sometimes NUDE WALK)   *noun.* Nudespeak for walking with no clothes on, saving always, of course, stout boots.

'North Yorkshire NUDE WALK. A North Yorkshire antiques expert tells me his favourite walk takes six hours and he is so confident that only the curlews and kestrels will be observers that he leaves his shorts in the car and walks completely nude apart from footwear. Lengthy details. SASE please.' (An entry in *Inland Free Sun*, 1988)

I think the curlews should be warned about the lengthy details.

O

OFFICIAL SECRETS

noun. Secrets that would embarrass a government if the public learnt that foreign powers had long been privy to them. (See DISINFORMATION and MANAGED NEWS.)

OFFICIAL SECRETS ACT

noun. Wise legislation to bring civil servants, who might otherwise become overmighty, into disrepute by forcing them to appear ignorant of matters which are common knowledge.

OFFSHORE

adjective. Beyond the prying impertinence of the revenue authorities.

OLIGOPOLISTIC

adjective. Forming an Oligopoly. A favourite among economists and bankers. Enough residual literacy persists among such people to warn them that 'monopoly' is not an accurate word for a small number of powerful institutions cornering all the loot. For some reason 'freemasonry' 'cartel', 'ring', 'log-rolleropoly', and 'conspiracy' all fail to commend themselves, and 'Oligopoly' gets the nomination.

'The fear that this would promote a few OLIGOPOLISTIC megabanks is unfounded ...' (*The Economist*, 14.2.87)

Why not 'The fear that this would benefit a few large banks ...'?

ONE-TO-ONE

noun and *adjective.* As in ONE-TO-ONE relationships. Californian CARE jargon for any sexual partnership that maintains its

165

exclusiveness for more than a week or two.

'Welcome to a new kind of weekly, collectable series. ONE-TO-ONE explores every aspect of the intimate relationships that really matter with a frankness you've always wanted.' (Publisher's blurb in a weekly 'partwork' magazine *ONE-TO-ONE* Orbis Publishing Ltd, February 1988)

What the copywriter is really saying to the audience is – 'AIDS is in. Swinging is out. So here's a magazine to reconcile you to this dull state of affairs.'

ON-GOING

adjective. A term used to suggest continuity where continuity cannot exist, as in 'on-going crisis'.

ONLY

adverb. Many otherwise clear sentences are made less clear by misplacing the words ONLY and 'even'. This error is so common that it seems pedantic to correct it, since the user's meaning is usually obvious to a sympathetic reader. But every loss of precision reduces the capacity of the language to express exact shades of difference, and there are some quarters to which one looks for support in small matters of syntax like this.

'When it comes to the crunch, many of your writers will ONLY be able to take the job so far (perhaps to first draft stage) and no further.' (*Clarity Begins at Home* a pamphlet advertising the services of the Plain English Campaign)

The sentence should read: ' ... many of your writers will be able to take the job ONLY so far ...'

OPERACY

noun. The word 'operation' is itself, in most of its modern guises, a good indicator of nonsense, but OPERACY is in a different class altogether. It dwells not in the vulgar world of action, but in the exalted realms of thought.

> 'Schools have always concerned themselves with numeracy and literacy and that remains the preoccupation of the new Bill. Yet "OPERACY" (the skills of doing) is every bit as important for most youngsters.' (Edward de Bono, letter to *The Times*, 27.1.88)

There you have it, from the mouth of the master himself. Ah! Doing! And the skills thereof! How the intelligentsia yearns for them!

> 'The thinking of OPERACY is quite different [from description, analysis and critical thinking] and is concerned with objectives, priorities, values, alternatives, guessing, consequences, decision, conflict, and other people's views.' (*Ibid.*)

Modern schools are not famously concerned with numeracy and literacy, but Dr de Bono may well be right in saying that no more are they concerned with objectives, priorities, values, alternatives, guessing, consequences, decision, and conflict. Perhaps we should be taught all these things, but they seem a little vague. How would you teach consequences?

So OPERACY means 'the skills of doing'. Why do I categorise this as nonsense? Firstly, out of sheer high spirits I cannot resist having a go at Dr de Bono's vocabulary, which relies heavily on big, vague words like the list beginning 'objectives', and then comes down with a bump on bits of gaunt polytechnicese like 'the skills of doing'. Secondly, there is a contradiction at the heart of Dr de Bono's position. He proclaims and elaborates the delights of LATERAL THINKING and OPERACY, but does so using what he would call the 'tools' of logical and critical thinking, in his terms 'vertical thinking'. In other words he makes his case by using the advantages of the system he is attacking. It is like a general claiming a victory when all he has done is to collaborate with the enemy.

I suppose we should be grateful that we were spared 'operationalism'.

OPI

noun. Always remind musicologists that the plural of Opus is Opera. It perplexes them.

OPINION POLL

noun. A count of all the emptiest heads.

ORGANIC

adjective. Nurtured on night soil, not nitrates. Pertaining to the peculiarities of pigshit.

> 'According to the ORGANIC view, society was able to operate as a system because of its hierarchically ordered but interdependent parts.' (Leonore Davidoff, 'Class and Gender in Victorian England', a contribution to *Sex and Class in Women's History*, Ryan & Walkowitz, Routledge and Kegan Paul, 1983)

This is not pigshit, but bullshit. Why is such a view ORGANIC, inorganic, atomic, modular, cellular or anything else? What is society if not some form of hierarchy? How can its parts be anything other than interdependent? And surely she means 'sex' not 'gender'? But Ms Davidoff is a mere beginner when it comes to penetrating the mysteries of the ORGANIC.

' ... allegory and irony are thus linked in their common demystification of an ORGANIC world postulated in a symbolic mode of analogical correspondences or in a mimetic mode of representation in which fiction and reality could coincide.' (Paul de Man, 'The Rhetoric of Temporality', a contribution to *Blindness and Insight: Essays in the Rhetoric of Contemporary Criticism*, Methuen, London, 1983)

The closest I can get is 'Allegory and irony both debunk conventional views of the world', but I'm open to suggestions. It's almost a relief to get back to ORGANIC meaning merely 'the absence of ADDITIVES'.

ORGASM

noun. The crescendo of sexual feeling experienced by a woman. For some reason men do not have orgasms – probably because they don't deserve them – and have to make do with 'climaxes'.

ORIENTAL JEWS

noun. A term used to denote Jews of non-European origin resident in Israel. It is a curious misnomer, since most of the Jews in question originate in Morocco – many hundred miles to the *west* of Israel. What is meant is *coloured* Jews.

ORIENTATION

noun. The tendency to turn east when praying, common to Muslims and Marxists.

OUTREACH

noun. A gesture, but only a gesture, of intense CARE and CONCERN made by the socially AWARE to those of whom they are aware.

The London Borough of Camden employs a TRAVELLERS' OUTREACH Officer. I picture this official reaching out yearningly towards the encamped Romanies, like purity appealing to Strength on a Victorian monument. I hope the Romanies respond gratefully and with proper feeling.

(See TRAVELLER.)

OVERFLIGHT

noun. Flying where you didn't oughter, like Icarus. And, like Icarus, coming a cropper.

The modern Icarus was Gary Powers. He should have known better than to fly in a plane called *You Too.* But you don't have to be spying to commit the sin of OVERFLIGHT. Any aircraft flying too close to the sun of Radar-Linked Surface-to-Air and Air-to-Air Enhanced Weapons Delivery Systems is asking to have its wax melted.

OVERKILL

noun. The serious military crime of using more projectiles than absolutely necessary to kill or incapacitate your opponent.

P

PACKAGE, THE: *noun.* An abstract collective noun used to suggest that more is on offer than is actually the case. 'The PACKAGE includes ...' and 'An attractive salary PACKAGE ...' are formulae that hint at cornucopian blessings. In fact they refer to matters like luncheon vouchers.

> 'The renumeration [*sic*] PACKAGE will reflect the seniority of this position, as well as experience and ability. It is not expected to be an obstacle.' (Advertisement in *The Times*, 14.1.88, for someone to undertake 'risk management' for Futures and Options)

No-one has ever offered me a job by prefacing his overtures with the undertaking that the *remuneration* PACKAGE will be no obstacle, and I feel correspondingly bitter. Indeed this PACKAGE is so UP-MARKET that it probably *does* include a spot of cornucopiana in the shape of cars and subsidised school fees.

Strictly speaking, 'remuneration' does not apply only to cash, since it derives from the Latin for 'gifts', but in English it carries a strong implication of 'payment'. Driving it in harness with PACKAGE, therefore, reduces the impact of PACKAGE, which is intended to suggest more than mere money.

In any case, either the word PACKAGE or the word 'remuneration' is unnecessary here, even when CREATIVELY spelt.

PAEDOCRACY

noun. Not 'government by children', but 'making children of adults' or 'assuming that adults are children'.

'Audiences are PAEDOCRATIZED to serve these needs. For the industry, television is a PAEDOCRATIC regime. The audience is imagined as having childlike qualities and attributes.' (John Hartley, 'Invisible fictions, TELE-VISION audiences, PAEDOCRACY, pleasure', an article in *Textual Practices*, summer 1987)

Textual Practices is a highbrow journal. It is produced from Cardiff University. Its editorial board is drawn from Oxford, universities in Canada, Australia, and the USA, and somewhere called Cambridge. John Hartley himself performs an undisclosed function at Murdoch University in Western Australia.

The burden of Mr Hartley's argument seems to be this. Television companies invent fictions about their audiences to justify the sort of programmes they want to broadcast. For fifteen pages he labours this point under sub-headings like 'PAE-DOCRATIC regimes', 'Family-circular arguments', and 'Regimes of pleasure'. He illustrates a pronounced characteristic of modern nonsense – the tendency to make mountains out of molehills, to exhaust elementary points, to flounder about in a humourless morass of self-importance.

To use PAEDOCRATISE as a transitive verb to indicate the tendency of broadcasters to take the lowest common denominator of the public's intelligence is overdramatic and tendentious. Besides, it's hideous.

It seems amazing that the editor of this journal did not spot the close euphony of

Textual Practices with 'sexual practices', and PAEDOCRACY with 'paedophilia'. Is the whole thing, perhaps, some element in the nationwide CHILD ABUSE scandal, written in an elaborate code?

PAINTERLY VALUES   *noun.* A smokescreen term used by ART critics to disguise the disgraceful fact that some artists can still draw.

In case you should think that I am flogging a dead horse, and that the ART crit world has long since sweated out the fevers of modernism, here is a scathing criticism of the exhibition '*Art of Our Time*' at the Scottish Royal Academy in 1987.

'One of the more pathetic claims made for this show is that it vindicates Scottish ART education. The ostrich that never noticed Modernism, let alone its critique, and went on for years drumming archaic drawing skills into a student body itself made complacent by its own conservative isolation, is turned into a virtue.' (Paul Wood, 'Exemplary Exhibitions', in *artscribe*, January 1988)

To teach artists to draw is as irrelevant as to teach art critics to write, and both malpractices should be stamped out.

Can you turn an ostrich into a virtue? It seems cruel.

PARENTING   *noun.* Unnecessary synonym for 'parenthood'. Perhaps PARENTING sounds more active and 'doing' than parenthood, and thereby commends itself to those who concern themselves with other people's responsibilities to their children. Or perhaps the distinction is that only one parent is involved in PARENTING, while it takes two for parenthood.

The woman's magazine *Spare Rib* has a whole page enitled PARENTING, which yields this example.

'We were the organisers of the Exploring Parenthood WORKSHOP, 'PARENT-ING Alone' at which Lisa Saffron had such an unpleasant time ...' (John Ballat and Anne Mhlongo, *Spare Rib*, January, 1988)

Obviously some sort of free fight broke out in the WORKSHOP, because while the writers 'unreservedly support Lisa's right to be a lesbian mother and to assert her identity anywhere she pleases', they go on: 'we do feel we have a responsibility to make things *safe* and productive for WORKSHOP participants'.(My italics)

One pictures the scene. Lisa asserts her identity as a lesbian mother. Someone else asserts *her* identity as a transexual parent. Remarks are passed. High words exchanged. One thing leads to another and – WALLOP!

But then, that's what PARENTING's all about.

PARTNER

noun. 1. One who shares your confidence in the hope of sharing your capital. TO FORM A PARTNERSHIP: To consort with known businessmen.

2. PARTNER has become the 'preferred' term to indicate the person with whom you live in some form of sexual relationship outside marriage. 'Mistress' and 'lover' are out of date (although a surprising number of women make the Jane Austen-like boast that they 'have a lover' – but with how different an emphasis). 'Common-law wife' sounds a bit cold. 'Boyfriend' and 'girl-friend' are widespread, but can be awk-

ward where homosexual relationships are concerned. No. It all comes down to PARTNER. All very clean and healthy. Like a game of tennis.

Anyone for mixed doubles?

PASSIVE SMOKING

verbal noun. The crime of being in the company of smokers. The passive smoker is at once a victim and a villain. As a stick with which to beat smokers, the sufferings of the passive smoker cannot be ignored. At the same time the vile fellow is actually to be found in the same company as smokers, and the zealots of the anti-smoking lobby are compelled to draw aside the hems of their garments from him, since he is indelibly contaminated. They treat him rather as a nervous missionary might treat a leper.

PATRIOTISM

noun. Patriotism is not enough. You've got to hate *everybody*.

PEACE AND NUCLEAR AFFAIRS OFFICER

noun. An official of the London Borough of Lambeth, charged with the heavy duty of persuading the USSR to exempt Lambeth from its plans for nuclear war – doubtless on the grounds that the borough harbours the headquarters of the Anglican Church, a notorious KGB front organisation.

PEACE STUDIES

noun. Studies in aid of the Soviet war effort.

PEER

noun. 1. A member of the House of Lords.

2. A term used by educational psychologists, in phrases like 'peer group pressure', to indicate the ruffianly behaviour of children left unsupervised.

The connection is surely obvious.

PEOPLE

adjective. Compassionately concerned with people, PERSONNEL, or HUMAN RESOURCES.

'We're a PEOPLE company'. (*Building Communications for Business*, a British Telecom instruction manual)

The implication of this usage is that 'We CARE'. It also suggests that British Telecom has a high level of camaraderie, and is a ball to work for. The folksy, deliberately-incorrect PEOPLE is deployed as an adjective to conjure up horrible visions of British Telecom tea rooms, and cheerful banter on the switchboard.

A widening usage, even to be heard in forms like 'I'm a PEOPLE person', meaning 'I'm sociable'.

PEOPLE'S

possessive adjective. Belonging to an unelected oligarchy.

PERIOD HOUSE

noun. With brilliant concision estate agents are able to summarise the whole history of architecture as either MODERN or PERIOD. But it is difficult to decide into which category a building falls when the estate agent describes it as 'expressing Tudor characteristics'.

'A superb new house with many PERIOD-style features'. (Advertisement by Chancellors and Co., *Country Life*, 26.2.87)

'Superb', in the sense of having overweening pride, this pretentious building certainly is. Perhaps one of its PERIOD-style features is to 'express Tudor characteristics' though the picture suggests a mock-Georgian rather than a mock-Elizabethan folly.

And:

'A superb Victorian cottage in North Battersea, beautifully presented ...' (Advertisement by John D. Wood & Co. in *Country Life*, 19.11.87)

If the word 'superb' has any meaning, it cannot possibly refer to a Victorian cottage in Battersea. How, in any case, do you 'present' a cottage, be it never so superb?

PERSONNEL

noun. Safely de-humanised employees. The collective noun for the faceless slaves of modern commerce.

PERSONNEL CARRIER

noun. A steel black maria employed by the military to eliminate the battlefield phenomenon of sudden unilateral withdrawal.

PERSONNEL DEPARTMENT

noun. The buffer between the greed of management and the grievances of its employees.

PERSPECTIVE

noun. The setting in which your own defects are viewed. IN PERSPECTIVE: viewed as leniently as possible.

PERSPECTIVE, with its implications of accurate drawing, is also a great favourite as a synonym for 'view', 'point of view', or 'attitude'.

'*Language and Learning: An interactional PERSPECTIVE.*' (Title of a book edited by Gordon Wells and John Nicholls, the Falmer Press, London, 1985)

The 'interaction' is between language and learning. The PERSPECTIVE is, presumably, the editors', or the contributors'.

PICKET

verb. To riot, brawl, cause an affray, or to create mayhem. The British lower orders, whose rulers have failed to maintain the former national diet of Frenchmen, Germans, and disaffected aborigines, have hit upon the PICKET LINE as a surrogate outlet for their warlike spirit.

PLANNER *noun.* One who sets in motion the random and chaotic forces of modernism. One under whose general direction motorways encroach, suburbs sprawl and airports proliferate.

'Milton Keynes is the fastest growing urban development in the UK. The Development Corporation's major task over the next few years is the promotion and development of Central Milton Keynes ... PLANNER ... £10,830-£11,856 ... we are looking for a strongly-motivated PLANNER ... ' (Job advertisement for a PLANNER in the *Guardian*, 6.1.88)

What is an 'urban development' if not a town? What is a 'MOTIVATED PLANNER' if not an enthusiastic vandal? The name *Central* Milton Keynes, implying that outlying areas exist or are planned, is deeply threatening. Have you ever *seen* Milton Keynes? It is indescribably horrible, embodying the chirpily-coloured-girder school of modern planning. For many years Milton Keynes has been at the centre of an artistically-devised advertising campaign, an unmistakable sign that there is something radically wrong with the place. No-one has to be persuaded to live in Florence or Venice. There is, of course, everything wrong with the place. It plays the monster to the PLANNERS' Frankenstein.

The first town PLANNER was the Emperor Nero.

PLURAL RELATIONS   *noun.* A euphemism dreamt up by the Boers – not normally a fanciful people – for the practice of APARTHEID. Under APART-HEID, naturally, anything more than a racially singular relationship is visited with condign severity.

PO   No part of speech; possibly a noun. The key, or trigger word of the LATERAL THINKER. Just as a child will shout 'Mummy, I'm ready!' when it wants its bottom wiped, so the LATERAL THINKER will exclaim 'PO!' when he has had an idea, or, better still, a CONCEPT.

> 'Just as "no" is the operative word of logical thinking, so the invented word 'PO' is the operative tool of LATERAL THINKING.' (Dr Edward de Bono, *Wordpower*, 1977)

> The wild cerebral frolics that Dr de Bono encourages deserve a more resounding and less suggestive catalyst than 'PO'. Dr de Bono is Maltese but, with the Royal Navy's long occupation of his island, there is no excuse for his not knowing that PO already has a perfectly good meaning in English.

> Perhaps when the conceptual block eases and the CONCEPTS begin to flow, the adoring LATERALISTS should all chant: 'Professor! We're ready!'.

> (See also CONCEPT, and LATERAL THINKING)

POINT OF SALE   *noun.* Where the CONSUMER and the PRODUCT are at long last united. POINT OF SALE is very popular because it implies precise knowledge in whoever is speaking, almost as if he has identified the very square foot on which the sale is made.

There it is! For one breathless second, time and space merge and stand still at the POINT OF SALE. But then the deed is done, the PRODUCT is entrusted to the CONSUMER, the CONSUMER's money to the salesman, and time resumes her inexorable progress.

The POINT OF SALE is, of course, a lazy way of avoiding a difficulty. The difficulty is that things are sold in a variety of different places – shops, markets, pubs, garages, emporia, stores, and so on. Rather than cudgel his brains to remind himself where the PRODUCT eventually turns up, a writer dealing with the MARKETPLACE falls limply back on POINT OF SALE.

POLITICIAN

noun. One who goes wherever the electorate follows.

POLLSTER

noun. The 20th century's Haruspex. One skilled in divining future events by inspecting not the entrails of chickens, but their utterances and opinions. (See OPINION POLLS.) Modern Haruspication has reached dizzying heights of sophistication and accuracy, and has formed an unholy alliance with STATISTICS. Together these two disciplines are so accurate that in a two-party election the forecasts of POLLSTERS are right almost 20 per cent of the time.

POSING POUCH

noun. The common or garden jock-strap, unbelievably transmogrified into an item of glamour-wear for body-builders and male models.

POSITIONAL GOODS

noun. The component parts of the 'positional economy', and the agents of 'social scarcity'.

Economists use the words 'good' and 'goods' in an annoyingly general way, meaning not only commercial goods, but also almost any component of the economy, material or abstract. They use the word 'positional' to mean 'determined by position'.

POSITIONAL GOODS therefore are goods whose value is determined by their position – presumably their position in the economy.

What on earth is that supposed to mean? Their physical, geographical position? Their 'position' on the ladder of cost? Does the term POSITIONAL GOODS make us any the wiser about anything to do with these goods?

No. And nor is the following elaboration much help.

'In the area of the economy represented by POSITIONAL GOODS, growth in aggregate availabilities is unattainable since it is subject to the limits of social scarcity.' (Professor Fred Hirsch, *Social Limits to Growth*, Routledge and Kegan Paul, London, 1977)

Professor Hirsch's analysis of economic growth is this: traditional economic growth takes two forms – the growth of the 'material economy' (the plebs' share of the cake), and intense competition to get a chunk of the 'positional economy' (the nobs' slice). Even when saturated with desirable consumer goods, the have-nots will still envy the haves, because only they get access to the POSITIONAL GOODS. These are all the bits and pieces which can never exist in quantities adequate to satisfy everyone who wants them. They incude desirable material objects, like Georgian

Manor Houses, and less material objects of desire like the post of Prime Minister or perhaps Professor Hirsch's own professorship and research fellowships.

Few of these things are 'goods' in the commercial sense (still less in an ethical sense), and to lump them all together because they have some fancied connection in the 'economy' (itself an undefined abstraction) seems to me captious. They could all be called VRDTs (Very Rare and Desirable Things).

In this case the correct reading of the sentence quoted above would be:

'You can't increase the availability of very rare and desirable things beause they are very rare.'

But Professor Hirsch is an academic economist, and economists must use strong, chunky words like 'goods' to demonstrate that they retain the common touch. By coupling 'goods' with a modern computerish word like 'positional' they have clearly demonstrated their membership of the modern elect, even if they haven't hit off a very accurate name for goodies restricted by rarity.

It has only just occurred to me that economists might intend 'goods' in the slang sense of 'goodies', and that academic gravitas compels them to leave out the 'ie'. There is much to be said for this interpretation, particularly as it beautifully sets the tone and level of the social concerns to which they address themselves.

The double use of 'goods' – to mean both chattels and more vague benefits – is a good example of how the modern mind moves in its mysterious ways to concoct nonsense. It is particularly to be savoured in the singular, thus:

> 'To the hungry man ... his meal is an entirely individual affair. In technical terms it is a private GOOD.' (*Ibid.* [There is an extraordinary weight of food imagery in economic writing – cake, pie, menu, slice])

The fact is that economics – like sociology and critical studies – is one of the half-disciplines. Its practitioners write badly because they are dealing in abstractions. I would suggest that they should all go back to school, but for the appalling fact that most of them would go back to the London School of Economics.

POSITIVE DIS-CRIMINATION

noun. Choosing applicants for a position on the grounds of race. It is quite distinct from RACIAL DISCRIMINATION, which is denying applicants a position on the grounds of race. (See BLACK.)

POST-MODERN

adjective. So new it's out of date already.

> 'The main themes of the first three-quarters of the book are a defence of some features of Modernism as a still ON-GOING project, the redescription of POST-MODERNISM is an epiphenomenon of Modernism itself, and an uneasiness over some of the theoretical underpinnings which have become fashionable in the ramified STRUCTURALISM of so much contemporary radical work. As such the outlook seems quite promising ...' ('Anglo-Stalinism', Paul Wood, *artscribe*, January 1988)

So promising that it is no surprise to learn a few lines later that:

> 'A caution over the totalising pretensions of STRUCTURALISM's epigones has been well-rehearsed.' (*Ibid.*)

So now we know what POST-MOD-ERNISM is. An 'Epiphenomenon' is an additional phenomenon, or, in medical terms, a secondary symptom. I like the medical analogy. Modernism is certainly a disease, with many disfiguring symptoms. There is no reason why POST-MOD-ERNISM should not be one of them.

POST-STRUC-TURALISM

*noun.*The heap of rubble left over after the collapse of STRUCTURALISM.

The POST-STRUCTURALISTS are not concerned with anything as mundane as language. The meaning of language is beneath them as well. But they come into their own with the meaning of the meaning of language, and on this they expend torrents of ink, shaped mostly into unreadable sentences like this:

> 'If, as Lacan argues, "no linguist or philosopher can maintain any longer a theory of language as a system of signs which doubles as a system of realities, the latter being defined by the common accord of sound minds in sound bodies", if the mutual recognition of subjects precedes the cognition of objects, this is because no fixation of linguistic meaning, no act of naming, can be accomplished in isolation from the system of language as a whole, and therefore from the continuous intersubjective co-ordination of language use which sustains this system.' (Peter Dews, *Logics of Disintegration, POST STRUCTU-RALIST Thought and the Claims of Critical Theory*, Verso Press, 1987)

Intense labour at the rock face can just about chisel this meaning out of Mr Dews's unyielding prose: 'The meaning of words cannot be taken in isolation from the traditions of language and its use.' This is scarcely a revolutionary INSIGHT into the meaning of language.

It is worth digressing for a moment into the phenomenon of Mr Dews, and why he chooses to express himself in the way he does. He is not a wholehearted POST-STRUCTURALIST. He has doubts. As the publisher's blurb informs us he 'draws on the INSIGHTS of Adorno to show how POST-STRUCTURALIST thought ultimately becomes entangled in the very "logic of disintegration" which it so vividly evokes'.

Disintegration indeed. The lengthy sentence quoted above is by no means exceptional. Most of Mr Dews's book is written like this. Nor is Mr Dews exceptional. Droves of supposedly educated people write like this. Where do they learn, or fail to learn, to write English?

In Mr Dews's case we must return to his publisher's blurb, which is simultaneously frank and reticent on the subject. No mention is made of Mr Dews's schooling, but we are told that 'he read for a first degree in English at Queen's College, Cambridge'. Did he get it? Internal evidence suggests that he did, because in his foreword he refers to a 'postgraduate' teaching job. After this he 'studied literary theory and philosophy at the Universities of Essex, Southampton and Paris ... and is currently lecturer in European Thought and Literature at Cambridgeshire College of Arts and Technology'.

I think these horrid revelations adequately explain Mr Dews' difficulties with English words.

But there are additional reasons, and they lie in the nature of his subject matter. POST-STRUCTURALISM is a develop ment of STRUCTURALISM, which originated as a method of analysing the origins of language. As soon as people began to look at this subject it became clear that children possess a command of the forms of language that exceeds anything they could have picked up from the limited vocabulary to which they have been exposed at that stage. It seemed, therefore, that there must be an underlying structure to language common to all mankind. This is the 'structure' of STRUCTURALISM.

But if there's a structure behind language, why not behind all behaviour – indeed behind everything? And since it is unidentified, speculative and invisible, we can invent it all, *and* all the attendant terminology and make an entirely new academic discipline, and endow chairs, and get tenure, and generally live the life of old Reilly.

STRUCTURALISM is a strongly determinist philosophy. If there are immutable underlying structures to everything, the human element in history and society can be discounted. (And if any of you, like me, can hear the dark pinions of Charles Darwin thrashing just off-stage, for God's sake don't mention it. The idea that the innate grasp of language shown by children might be genetically determined is out, out, out.)

It didn't take the STRUCTURALISTS long to work out that since different languages use different words for identical objects, then the actual word is an arbitrary choice, with no essential connection with its object. And since the word possesses no innate qualities, how are we to be sure that the object does? Surely everything exists only in relation to the other things around it?

What on earth have we got now? Relativist Determinism by the looks of it.

Like all relativist arguments, the STRUCTURALIST argument disappears up its own behind. If words are arbitrary signs which depend for their meaning on surrounding arbitrary signs, and if all previous thinking is rendered invalid for this reason, then what is the value of the acres of turgid prose spread out by the STRUCTURALISTS before our appalled gaze?

None, but that alone would have been no deterrent to the progress of STRUCTURALISM. What finally torpedoed it, and ushered in POST-STRUCTURALISM, was a far more serious matter.

As the STRUCTURALISTS burrowed away like aardvarks, throwing up an immense spoil-heap of verbiage behind them, the awareness grew on them –

'Are we not, with our synchronic STRUCTURALIST METHODOLOGY, pursuing a mode of analysis fundamentally opposed to MARXISM, with its diachronic mode of analysis? Are we good leftists?'

This tormented doubt had all the tragedy of a Catholic losing his faith. In the 1960s, when this development occurred, such a consideration was unbearable. Immediately a task force of French *enragés* leapt into the breach. Working in shifts round the clock this gallant band – Jacques Derrida, Jacques Lacan, Jean-François Lyotard, and Michel Foucault – restored the radical purity of their discipline by re-identifying it as POST-STRUCTURALISM (sometimes 'deconstruction'). Contemptuously they dismissed Husserlian Phenomenology. Clinically they dissected *Différence* and the Regress of Reflection. How piercingly did Lacan lay bare Language, Subjectivity and Historicity. What subtle resonances did Lyotard bring to Discourse and its Other.

Finally, gasping, flushed, but triumphant, they planted their flag on the summit of their own massive spoil-heap of words, POST-STRUCTURALISM.

It seems churlish of Mr Dews to have any doubts.

I am aware that I have wandered almost as far as the POST-STRUCTURALISTS, and I must return to my starting point. Second to his education, his subject matter is responsible for Mr Dews' prose. In common with all the other half-disciplines, Critical Theory longs for the respectability of the hard sciences, but cannot tear itself away from the lush pastures of abstraction and speculation. You may indeed wonder how such a narrow subject as language manages to proliferate into every nook and cranny of philosophy, sociology, and politics. The explanation is the megalomania of the modern intellectual. He cannot resist the luxury of feeling that his subject underlies and permeates all others, and to enjoy this illusion he builds a tottering superstructure of jargon and nonsense.

Both STRUCTURALISTS and POST-STRUCTURALISTS embrace the view that the structure of language conditions the way in which people perceive the world around them. Since all supposedly objective perception is in fact conditioned by the subjective structure of language there is no true objectivity, and the only people who hold the key to TRUTH are those who have mapped out this structure. Guess who?

This is so obviously a philosophy of convenience that it should be dismissed out of hand on those grounds alone. But the aficionado of the modern mind should be grateful, because in their attempts to assert the primacy of their discipline in every field, the STRUCTURALISTS and POST-STRUCTURALISTS have brought modern nonsense to its finest and most voluminous flowering.

POVERTY TRAP

noun The inexorable process by which the poor get poorer, and the rich get richer. Legislative attempts to remedy this result in the poor getting poorer and the rich getting poorer.

PRE-EMPTIVE STRIKE

noun. A surprise attack. For obvious reasons this has always been a favourite tactic among warmongers, but it is plainly 'unfair' and 'against the rules'. It is therefore more soothing to dress up your surprise attack as a PRE-EMPTIVE STRIKE. Lord Nelson brought off a very creditable PRE-EMPTIVE STRIKE against the mighty Danes at Copenhagen, and the Japanese deserve an honourable mention for a spirited attempt at Pearl Harbor.

PRE-OWNED

adjective. Second-hand, but better than second-hand. 'Second-hand' is not far from a pejorative, and also carries echoes of 'second-rate'. PRE-OWNED, however, is reassuringly positive, almost AFFIR-MATIVE.

Would you buy a PRE-OWNED car from a man who used the expression?

PRESTIGIOUS

adjective. This is almost invariably used to mean 'having fame or renown', and not, as it should, 'having sleight of hand, light-fingered, thieving'. Often corporations or companies are described as PRESTIGIOUS with unintentional candour. Here is an example without such overtones, but enlivened by a delightful misspelling.

'Minster Lovell, Oxfordshire. A PRE-STIGEOUS conference centre situated in the beautiful Windrush Valley ...' (Advertisement by Hampton & Sons, *Country Life*, 26.2.87)

The advertisement incudes this sentence, given in its entirety: 'The winner of a European Architectural Award and set in beautiful grounds of about 50 acres alongside the River Windrush.' Grammar aside, all who remember the mill at Minster Lovell before European Award-winning architects got hold of it, must wonder where the prestige, except in the sense of nimble-fingeredness, comes in.

'A distinguished West German historian with controversial views on the Holo-caust last night described the sudden withdrawal of an invitation to contri-bute to a PRESTIGIOUS series of lectures at Wolfson College, Oxford, as irrational and disappointing.' (Simon Midgley, the *Independent*, 24.10.88) (See DISINVITE.)

Wolfson College could perhaps ENHANCE the PRESTIGIOUSNESS of its lectures by making use of the Minster Lovell conference centre.

And here is PRESTIGIOUS in a context so delicate that it is difficult to decide if it is meant in its corrupt sense or in its correct sense.

'Mr David Mayhew, a partner in Cazenove & Co., the most prestigious firm of stockbrokers in the City was arrested yesterday and charged wih three offences arising out of the Guinness affair.' (A report in *The Times*, 8.4.88)

PREVENTIVE INITIATIVE (also PREVENTIVE ACTION or WAR)

noun. Invasion, attack, assault, onslaught, irruption, conquest or annexation. A close relative of PRE-EMPTIVE STRIKE, but altogether a more ritualised, ordered and permanent affair. The oldest and favourite excuse for attacking and conquering your neighbour – 'He was about to do it to me!'

PREVENTIVE MEDICINE

noun. Of itself an obviously useful idea, PREVENTIVE MEDICINE can unfortunately be extended to embrace all forms of prevention within spitting distance of the HEALTH industry. It is the umbrella under which the modern puritan seeks to outlaw all pleasurable activity on the general ground that it might in the long run be bad for you. In this he does no more than elaborate the age-old axiom that life is very bad for you – culminating as it invariably does in death. The rallying cry of a hideous tribe of goody-goodies who dislike meat, drink, tobacco, or any form of vigorous or extrovert activity.

PRIMARY SOURCES

plural noun. History written by interested parties, and for that reason more palatable to modern historians than secondary sources, or history written by historians.

PRIVATISATION

noun. The selling of publicly-owned concerns to the public. Only the state could get away with such a bare-faced piece of fraud. The state concern that will never be privatised, however, is the one area in which government is more efficient than the private sector – organised crime. The exactions of the state far exceed the depradations of private sector criminals – nor is it possible to insure against them.

PROACTIVE

adjective. A business term meaning 'we go out there and get stuck in'. A hopeless, wet businessman who sat waiting for business to come to him would be 'reactive'. INNOVATIVE, CREATIVE businessmen are PROACTIVE.

PRODUCT, THE

noun. Modern commerce has deteriorated to such an extent that what you manufacture can never be named for fear of exposing its inadequacies. This applies particularly among those charged with advertising and selling THE PRODUCT, who shrink from naming it in the superstitious way that actors shrink from saying Macbeth. So great is their horror of actuality that THE PRODUCT itself has become suspect, and is often subsumed in a still greater abstraction, THE PACKAGE.

PROSPERITY CONCEPT

noun. (See CONCEPT.) An idea for making money.

'The 18 year old Sausalito restaurant worker asserted that "it's not a chain letter. It's a PROSPERITY CONCEPT. I know the people involved in it and I trust them. They're good people, very conscious in dealing with the higher consciousness of money".' (A report in the *San Francisco Sunday Examiner & Chronicle*, 25.9.78., on the Chain Letter craze)

The 'Chain of Gold' letter is itself worth quoting. Bear in mind that the purpose of this letter is to separate you from $100.

'A friend of yours who believes in the freedom to give and receive unlimited quantities of love wishes to share this belief with you in the tangible form of financial abundance.' (*Ibid.*)

California here I come.

PROTESTANT WORK ETHIC   *noun.* The obsession of Protestants with busy irrelevancies to divert attention from the sketchy nature of their religious observances. The displacement activity of the guilty. The Protestant substitute for confession, with confessional, confessor and penance all rolled into one.

PROVOCATION   *noun.* The presence of the police in any ratio exceeding one in twenty to potential trouble makers. Any opposition – even in the form of dumb insolence – to the demands, arguments and aspirations of the left.

PSYCHOANALYSIS   *noun.* Dropping a pebble into the well of unconsciousness and inferring from the splash what decaying matter is swilling about in the water.

PUB GRUB   *noun.* A fragment of ancient English, believed to be an abusive answer to the conundrum: 'Which came first, the chicken or the basket?' (See MICROWAVE.)

PUBLIC   *adjective.* Another versatile word which, in England, entirely reverses its meaning when followed by the word 'school'.

PUBLIC RELATIONS   *noun.* The art of deploying between your paymaster and the public a dense smoke-screen of lies.

Q

QUAFFABLE

adjective. The quality of a wine so bad that only flinging it back with desperately assumed good cheer makes it possible to swallow at all.

> 'From QUAFFABLE plonk to the finest Burgundies', (list of Les Caves de Ma Grand Mère Ltd., 20 Bedford Street, London. September 1987)

The combination of a Falstaffian word like QUAFFABLE and a blunt polytechnic monosyllable like 'plonk' is especially ridiculous, even among the excesses of Wine Blurbese. The writer is signalling to his readers – 'Look. This is little better than Algerian axle grease, but if you swallow it fast enough you won't notice the taste. Besides, never mind the quality, feel the price.'

The eye-rhyme with 'affable' makes this a much-prized word in wine circles, where sympathetic human qualities are always looked for in the wine being tasted. If they have not been found by the bottom of the second bottle, it is usually too late.

QUANTUM LEAP

noun. The QUANTUM is a merry little quadruped, similar to the chamois of Europe and the klipspringer of Africa, and, like them, noted for its agility. The QUANTUM's chief habitat is the tangled interior of a physicist's head, where its incessant frolicking causes much CEREBRAL disturbance, stimulating many wild associations of ideas. Hence QUANTUM LEAP.

R

RACE RELATIONS

noun. A profession dedicated to improving relations between the races by advertising the iniquities of the least fashionable group.

> 'Race and Housing team: We need people with ideas and drive to lead the housing service's anti-racist strategy. The team will be located in the Housing Department but will have strong functional links with the Central Race Equality Unit.' (Advertisement placed in the *Guardian*, 6.1.88., by the London Borough of Ealing)

Five jobs were listed below this preamble: a Principal Race Equality Officer; a Race Equality Officer; another Race Equality Officer; a Policy and Research Assistant; and a Training Co-ordinator (Housing). The total yearly cost of these officials to the Ealing ratepayers – even at the lowest salaries quoted – would be £77,874.

The duties of these officers include: ethnic monitoring, developing an anti-racist strategy, analysing training needs, and developing a POSITIVE ACTION training programme.

And this is only the *housing* race team. How many other 'race officers' flourish under the protection of the Ealing Council? And what do they do, other than foment dissatisfaction among 'ethnic minority groups'?

Because it is important to note that RACE RELATIONS are a one-way trade.

It is *only* the minority groups that attract the attention of Race Equality Officers. Discrimination practised by the minorities on the majority (who might easily be in a local minority) does not count. A majority in the RACE RELATIONS industry would probably deny that such discrimination could occur, because such people are seldom students of human nature, preferring, like the Boers, to see things in BLACK and white.

[Besides, all sectarian and racial problems are only partly sectarian and racial. If you removed all the males of one community, and all the females of the other, your problem would be solved in under a week.]

Keep an eye on that phrase 'ethnic monitoring'. It has a nasty 1984-ish ring to it.

RACISM   *noun.* A contraction of 'racialism', dear to the modern mind because it sounds more like FASCISM. The atrocious error of supposing that there is any difference between a Hottentot and a Lapp. (See BLACK and POSITIVE DISCRIMINATION.)

RANDOMISATION   *noun.* The means by which statisticians attempt to simulate disorder in an orderly manner.

RAPID OXIDATION   *noun.* Fire. Combustion. Used when fire threatened to engulf the Three Mile island nuclear power station in the USA. The idea of a nuclear reactor on fire was too alarming for public consumption. All that had happened was a slight case of RAPID OXIDATION.

**REAL TERMS/IN
REAL TERMS**

noun. A usage of startling candour, which concedes that monetary terms are not real.

REFERENDUM

noun. A plebiscite purged of its embarrassing working-class associations, and consequently much in favour with Social Democrats and Liberals.

**REPRESSIVE
TOLERANCE**

noun. A term coined by Herbert Marcuse to explain how very intolerant it is to allow people to do what they want.

By allowing people to do what they want, you encourage them to develop 'FALSE CONSCIOUSNESS', which is a left-wing way of saying 'ambition'. They will aspire – drat them. And if some of these aspirations are to some extent met, they will continue to aspire, and others likewise.

It is unthinkably unproletarian to aspire. And since to be proletarian is the highest state of human attainment, if you tolerate non-proletarian aspirations, you are repressing the right to be proletarian. There are similarities here with the notion of AFFIRMATIVE culture (see AFFIRMATIVE), and perhaps even the Catholic practice of confession should be seen as a form of REPRESSIVE TOLERANCE.

Marcuse is really lamenting the efficiency of democratic societies in supplying both material and immaterial needs. While they continue to do so, their opponents will continue to be compelled to fall back on contradictory nonsense like REPRESSIVE TOLERANCE to justify their aversion to what is obviously a desirable state of affairs.

REPRESSIVE TOLERANCE is particularly relevant to FREE SPEECH. To allow people to express their opinions in speech and writing, without any fear of the consequences, is the most blatant and obvious form of oppression. It is solely to provide a 'safety valve' so that the 'revolutionary consciousness' of the people shall be blunted.

Marcuse was a refugee from Hitler's Germany who taught in several American universities, including Harvard. It is charitable to conclude that falling out of the frying pan of the Holocaust into the fire of American campus life unseated his reason. His theories about the fraudulence of DEMOCRACY, the illusion of freedom, and the necessity for revolutionary violence and terror, are not far from being unhinged. But in the 60s and 70s he built up an immense and fashionable following, and thereby earns his place in a dictionary of modern nonsense.

RESTRUCTURATION *noun.* A method or methods of rearranging a company's financial affairs, carefully left unspecified.

> 'EMM Group, SA. Financial Service Division. Specialists in Corporate Finance, RESTRUCTURATION, Acquisitions, and Mergers.' (*Financial Times*, 13.10.87)

Those wishing to avail themselves of the EMM Group's services might well be trying to organise a LEVERAGED MANAGEMENT BUY OUT.

RETINAL EXPERIENCE *noun.* What Californians have instead of sight.

RETOOL *verb.* An engineering works that was overhauling its equipment could be said to be RETOOLING. The suggestion of the rugged world of engineering is too much for the ART crit boys, who have taken RETOOL to their collective bosom.

Another discipline talks of 'tooling' leather, and perhaps a very weary piece of leather, coming round for the second time, could be said to be RETOOLED.

I am not sure to which of these derivations we owe this:

> 'Ettore Sottsass's new furniture RETOOLS the Memphis design esthetic with an upscale grandeur.' (Brook Adams, writing in *ART in America*, February, 1988)

It is worth noting in passing that the American ART crit biz has decided to spell AESTHETIC 'esthetic'. O Oscar! Thou shouldst be living at this hour! The idea that Memphis is the home of any AESTHETIC, however debased, is bizarre in the extreme. Perhaps it is merely a generic title for a school of furniture design, deriving, not from Tennessee, but from ancient Egypt. I have not enquired.

'Upscale' is very good. It appears to be an adjective qualifying 'grandeur'. I looked hard at Signor Sottsass's furniture, but was unable to say to what extent his grandeur is upscale.

REVOLUTION *noun.* A faction-fight by a group so small and unrepresentative that it can attain power only after the parent country has been reduced to chaos and breakdown, a state of affairs that must therefore be the group's first aim.

REVOLUTIONARY *noun.* One who, with much unnecessary fuss, devotes his political energies to bringing matters full circle.

RIGHTS

noun. The unnegotiable currency in which politicians pay for votes. Things were better ordered in the 18th century when the buggers had to pay in cash, or at the very least in beer.

'STUFF YOUR LOANS! EDUCATION is a RIGHT.' (A placard displayed by students during a demonstration against the suggestion that students should in due course repay their grants. London, 24.11.88)

EDUCATION is indeed one of the RIGHTS for so long dangled in front of the electorate by politicians. Or rather, *free* EDUCATION. But nothing is free, and the more intelligent and/or honest politicians qualify 'free' with the delicious appetiser 'free at the point of use'. The taxpayer foots the bill. (See TAXATION.)

The spectacle of thousands of young people clamouring for modern education as a RIGHT is so heartrending that perhaps some other form of education should be obligatory to correct these self-destructive urges.

The students seem to have been motivated more by principle than by financial duress, since the police reported that the demonstrators 'made a deliberate attack on a police cordon', hurling *coins*, bottles and cans.

RIGHTS obey the law of DISTRIBUTIONAL COMPULSION. The more basic RIGHTS you satisfy, the more perks and fringe benefits will be demanded as RIGHTS. Above all anything provided by your fellow taxpayers automatically becomes a RIGHT of the most entrenched kind – if only because politicians find it so easy to trade for your vote.

RIGHT TO CHOOSE *noun.* Infanticide. The RIGHT, claimed by women, to slay their unborn offspring.

- 'Stop the Alton Bill. Defend a Woman's RIGHT TO CHOOSE'. (A slogan printed in an advertisement placed by the General, Municipal, Boilermakers' and Allied Trades Union in *MARXISM TODAY* January,1988)

Boilermakers?

The Bill referred to was a measure introduced by the Liberal MP David Alton to reduce the minimum term at which an abortion may be procured from 28 weeks to 18. Alton is particularly detested by his opponents for being a man, single (often stigmatised as 'celibate', but what is their evidence?), and, worst of all, a Catholic.

Neither side finds it easy to be honest about abortion. The anti-abortionists, mainly Christian with a strong Catholic bias, would be on strong ground about the sin of murder and the sanctity of life, were it not for the fact that for centuries the churches have condoned war, judicial execution, and killing in self-defence. The uncomfortable fact is that abortion is connected with sex – a subject no Christian, never mind Catholic, finds it easy to be sensible about.

But the evasions of the antis pale into insignificance beside the pro-abortion lobby. They go to inordinate and comic lengths not to mention words like 'kill' and 'death'. They endlessly qualify the noun 'life' with adjectives like VIABLE, as if a child on the brink of popping out of the womb is in some way more 'VIABLE' than one with a few weeks to go. They gloss, or ignore, the fact that since the 1967 Act some three million unborn children have been killed. Picture their howls of rage if the Boers had cleaned up to even a quarter of that extent in the townships.

I have never killed anyone myself, but I am not one to spoil other people's fun. All history attests to our unconfined glee in slaughter. It is very SEXIST, Chauvinist, and prejudiced of Mr Alton to attempt to de-feminise death. Let women have their RIGHT, but let us call it by its correct name – the RIGHT TO KILL.

S

SEAMLESS

adjective. Critic-ese for a piece of writing or work of art so dull that no variation or any other point of interest can be detected on its uniform surface.

'Thus Professor Rosenblum's apparent assumption of a SEAMLESS and generalised – male – sexuality ... neither does service to Salle nor justice to a serious cultural or political criticism.' (Paul Wood, 'Exemplary Exhibitions', a contribution to *artscribe*, January 1988)

Surely sexuality must be male if it be SEAMLESS? I mean, that's how it's always seemed to me. With what is Professor Rosenblum being threatened in the word 'apparent'? Does it suggest that he hasn't *really* assumed this SEAMLESS, generalised, male sexuality? Is he, in reality a particularly fissured woman? Anyway, whatever his sexual identity, he has sacrificed his membership of the modern elect. He has failed to do justice to a serious cultural or political criticism.

SECURITISATION

noun. Not 'making a risk safe', but 'making yourself safe by getting rid of the risk'. A form of passing the buck and spreading the load. Assets, debts and mortgages can all be the objects of SECURITISATION. They are 'sold on' by the originating institution to others who feel more confident of their ability to 'manage the risk' – rather as IOUs used to be sold in the old days.

' ... SECURITISED debt has replaced more traditional forms of borrowing ... ' (Patrick Haverson writing in *ICB, International Banking*, August 1987)

'Like so many recent mortgage innovations, the idea of SECURI-TISATION originated in the US. It began with the thrift institutions who quickly realised that by SECURITISING their mortgages they could increase the availability of their mortgage funds and also increase their return on capital employed. It enabled them to concentrate on the profitable activity of providing loans, rather than the low margin business of carrying loans for a long period.' (Peter Jeffrey, *Ibid.*)

There are similarities here with LOSS ADJUSTMENT. Fleece the customer, and then pass your obligations on to some hard-nosed denizen of the financial underworld. The 'thrift institutions' are well named.

SECURITY RISK *noun*. The banner under which the modern puritan persecutes the few public figures still able to make the two-backed beast.

SELF CRITICISM *noun*. What Communists have instead of confession. Catholic power hunger usually stops short at the soul, and therefore confessions are heard in private. But Communist power hunger is not content without mind and body as well, and SELF CRITICISM is a public matter. Psychologically, SELF CRITICISM is very similar to 'owning up' at school – the desperate hope that a candid admission of fault will avert the full wrath of authority. It is a characteristic of tyrannies that they project into adult life the cruelties and injustices of childhood, and the mental atmosphere that attends them.

SELF-STARTER   *noun.* One craven enough to be daily up and doing at someone else's behest.

SELF-STYLED/SELF-APPOINTED   *adjective.* The quality of any position of merit, or claim to merit, attained by your opponent.

> 'The SELF-STYLED right-wing LIBER-TARIANS of the *Sunday Times* should be giving a lead ...' (Leader in *New Society*, 22.1.88)

It has never occurred to me before that the *Sunday Times* is a right-wing newspaper. It is noteworthy that the writer doesn't challenge the sincerity of the *Sunday Times*, as he would had he said 'so-called LIBERTARIANS'. 'SELF-STYLING' is an altogether more serious matter than hypocrisy. It is a form of *lèse majesté* – injuring the majesty of the left by invading its monopoly of libertarianism, which is now but a step removed from 'bourgeois individualism'.

SEMANTICS   *noun.* A branch of philology concerned with the meaning of words, and therefore a word most often used by those who do not know its meaning.

> 'If one cannot summarize dissemination, seminal differance [*sic*], in its conceptual tenor, this is because the force and form of its disruption burst the SEMANTIC horizon.' (Jacques Derrida, *Positions*, London 1981)

If a horizon can be burst, which I doubt, it is clear that M. Derrida has wallowed to excess in the consequent spate of meaninglessness.

SEMIOTICS

noun. The terse American equivalent of the flowery French 'semiology'. Both words name the science of signs. Because, with a spot of LATERAL THINKING, a sign can be anything from a rude gesture to a painting by an old master, SEMIOTICS have been warmly embraced by sociologists, POST-STRUCTURALISTS, and educational theorists. The science has, indeed, been largely subsumed in POST-STRUCTURALISM which loves to think of revered works of literature as no more than signs, leaving the POST-STRUCTURA-LISTS free to tell everyone what the signs mean.

> 'Social SEMIOTICS and the pragmatics of language development. The cognition hypothesis tended to focus attention on the difference between sensori-motor intelligence and subsequent thinking, with particular reference to Piaget's developmental theory.' (John Nicholls and Gordon Wells, *Language and Learning: an Interactional PERSPECTIVE*, the Falmer Press, 1985)

Drowning in theory and hypotheses, these linguistic analysts. But here is another theory of signs, equally hypothetical, but much more interesting.

The commonest sign known to the rude British is the V sign. It is taken to mean 'up yours', or something ruder. But why this should be is obscure. The gesture itself is not very suggestive. Here is the explanation.

During the Hundred Years War English longbowmen were regarded with particular aversion by the opposing French. When they were lucky enough to capture English archers, the French, recoiling from the sin of murder, merely severed the bow-string fingers of the archers' right hands, to put them out of action for ever. It therefore became the habit of the English archers to wave their bow-string fingers at their opponents whenever they met, to show them that they were intact and ready. From this the V sign developed into a general gesture of derision.

This story has the awful ring of likelihood, but I know of no evidence for it, and I can't even remember where I heard it.

That's SEMIOTICS for you.

SENSITIVE

adjective. A word that has subtly changed its meaning. No longer does it mean 'having sensitivity', but 'having qualities that might cause me sensitivity'. With this emphasis it has come to indicate anything potentially embarrassing.

> 'For British Telecom PERSONNEL only: commercially SENSITIVE' (A warning printed in *British Communications for Business*, a British Telecom instruction manual)

Presumably British Telecom means to say that competitors might profit by the contents of the booklet. Or possibly that the booklet reveals commercial practices that might cause BT embarrassment if known publicly. Either way the word SENSITIVE, from being a largely passive word – I am very SENSITIVE to criticism – has become active. The correct modern usage would be 'From a personal PERSPECTIVE, criticism is a very SENSITIVE area.'

> 'Safe, strong, and naturally SENSITIVE.' (Words printed on the packets containing *Mates*, the friendly condoms of the AIDS-conscious eighties)

The wearer of the condom may be SENSITIVE. His partner may be SENSITIVE. The condom may be so finely constructed that it does nothing to diminish this happy state of affairs. But it cannot possibly be SENSITIVE itself, particularly 'naturally' SENSITIVE.

A second brand of *Mates* drops the claim to SENSITIVITY entirely, and displays instead the word 'tough'. You pays your money and you takes your choice. I suppose it all depends what you want them for.

SEX EDUCATION

noun. The diversion of funds and effort into teaching the one human activity – apart, perhaps, from evacuating the bowels – that does not need to be taught.

SEXISM

noun. An inscrutable offence, unconsciously committed by men, and detectable only by women. The frightful crime of assuming that the differences between the sexes are there for our delight.

SEXUAL HARASSMENT

noun. The attentions of someone you do not find attractive.

SIDE-EFFECT

noun. An effect that sneaks up on you.

SILENT MAJORITY

noun. The imagined supporters of a vociferous minority.

SIMPLISTIC

adjective. A pretentious way of saying 'simple'. A 'simplist' used to be a herbalist, but those who use SIMPLISTIC nowadays mean only 'simple'.

' ... a disregard for the views of others as she prosecutes her own SIMPLISTIC Poujadist view of society.' (The Parliamentary column in *Tribune*, 8.1.88)

She, of course, is Mrs Thatcher. If you were to say that Mrs Thatcher's views were 'simple' it would lack the grand academic ring of SIMPLISTIC. The *Tribune* is not allowed to demonstrate class prejudice, otherwise it might just as well come clean and say that Mrs Thatcher is lower middle class. This is the most obvious quality she shares with Monsieur Poujade, whose political organisation was formed to fight against the French tax system. Would that Mrs T *were* more akin to M. Poujade. The lower middle classes as represented by the small businessman and the self-employed have not been freed by Mrs Thatcher from the heaviest burden under which free Britons have had to labour since the Bill of Rights – VALUE ADDED TAX.

SITUATION ETHICS   *noun.* Sired by casuistry out of sophistry, SITUATION ETHICS are what you take refuge in when you are obliged to justify your actions after the event. Cutting your ethical cloth to suit your pragmatic coat.

SLOANE RANGER   *noun.* A young English, or sometimes Scottish, woman of the upper, or near-upper, classes, in whom shyness and acute class-consciousness combine to defeat all attempts at communication, confiding her to strangled utterances like 'OK' and 'Ya'. This disability does not, in some unexplained way, spare her interlocutor from learning all about Mummy and Daddy and what a scream Nigel was après-skiing at Meribel.

These endearing ornaments of the British scene are an unfailing source of wonder to foreigners – especially Americans – who sometimes employ them as secretaries, with shattering consequences to their telephone bills.

SOCIALISM   *noun.* 1. The MORALITY of the irreligious.
2. The stalking horse of MARXISM.
3. The belief that the quickest way to end capitalism is unrestricted self-indulgence in its fruits.

SOCIALIST WORKERS PARTY   *noun.* A fissiparous and discordant group of drones.

SOCIAL OWNERSHIP   *noun.* The nationalisation of a CARING government.

SOCIAL SCIENCE   *noun.* Anti-social mumbo jumbo.

SOCIAL SECURITY   *noun.* To be on SOCIAL SECURITY is to occupy a position of extreme precariousness outside society.

SOCIO-ECONOMIC GROUP   *noun.* Class. The upper, upper-middle, middle, lower-middle and working classes have been replaced with SOCIO-ECONOMIC GROUPS 1,2,3,4, and 5. This has not always been to the advantage of progress and enlightenment. It is difficult to work up much SOCIO-ECONOMIC GROUP 5 solidarity.

SOFTWARE/ HARDWARE   *noun.* In a reversal of the normal sexual imagery, SOFTWARE is what you put in, and HARDWARE is what you put it into.

SPECTRUM   *noun.* A measure of width across the whole of which political analysts and opinion-seekers rampage without control.
Here is another SPECTRUM, equally comprehensively embraced.

'In short, our group is BROADLY-BASED across the SPECTRUM of information and entertainment.' (Mr

Rupert Murdoch, 1986 Annual Report of The News Corporation Ltd)

'I own lots of newspapers, magazines, and television stations' would have done just as well.

SPORTSMAN

noun. One trained to win at all costs, and skilled in the histrionics of losing. A being in whom the ego rules supreme, and finds expression in various otiose skills, often involving balls. A person who preserves all the pettishness of childhood into adult life. One whose unceasing threnody is 'I can do it, Mummy, I can do it!' And when he can't he hollers.

> 'More prosecutions should be launched against SPORTSMEN and women involved in violent attacks on each other during matches, the Criminal Injuries Compensation Board urged in a report published yesterday.' (Front page story in *The Times*, 10.12.87)

It is clear from this that SPORTSMAN has entirely lost the associations it used to have with fair play, polite conduct, and losing gracefully. In the old days *The Times* would have felt constrained to say 'so-called SPORTSMEN', or at the very least to put SPORTSMEN in inverted commas. But even The Thunderer now recognises that sport, once the collective noun for outdoor activities indulged in for fun and in accordance with a strict code of behaviour, has become the arena of all that is rancorous, petty and mean in the human spirit.

The sort of mind that needs the competitive outlets provided by sport, has, of course, always been rancorous, petty and mean. But in more civilised times such people were expected to put a good face on their primitive impulses. Their fixed smiles in defeat were much more diverting to the beholder than the tantrums of modern SPORTSMEN.

STAFF SHORTAGE

noun. Absenteeism. The excuse offered for a late or cancelled train service when the driver hasn't bothered to turn up for work.

STAND-ALONE

adjective. The state of being the lonely little petunia in the onion patch of technology. A STAND-ALONE computer is one not linked to a mainframe. By extension it refers to any self-contained system. An earth closet at the bottom of the garden is a STAND-ALONE ablutionary FACILITY.

STAND-BY CREDIT FACILITY

noun. A small, short-term loan, at very high interest, grudgingly extended to debtors so desperate that without this softener they might welsh on more lucrative repayments.

STATE OF THE ART

adjective, as in STATE OF THE ART computer. Used to describe the *dernier cri* in any field of technical development, but especially in those fields of development moving so fast that nothing is STATE OF THE ART for long. It does not apply, most emphatically, to the arts, but only to industry and technology. You cannot have a STATE OF THE ART painting, but you can have a STATE OF THE ART screwdriver.

'The quality of the refinements and STATE OF THE ART equipment, which comes as standard, achieve a level of finish rarely seen in London residential buildings.' (Copy in a brochure published to advertise flats in 'The Circle', a 'development' near Tower Bridge by the Jacob's Island Property Company)

Does this mean that both the refinements and the equipment achieve a level of finish, but only the equipment comes as standard? Do both the refinements and the equipment have quality, or just the refinements? Neither of these points is clear from the structure of the sentence, which is majestically awry. What is the subject of the verb 'achieve'? But we are left in no doubt about the STATE OF THE ART.

'The door handles and light switches are finished in brushed chrome ... polished chrome taps and accessoires [*sic*] ... sliding mirrored door fully fitted walk-in wardrobes ...' (*Ibid.*)

STATISTICS

noun. 1. Distilled essence of humbug.
2. The ART of clouding simple issues by injecting a lethal dose of mathematics.

STORYNESS

noun. The quality of having narrative form.

'Sensibly ignoring any "action sequence", which neo-Aristotelian analysts regard as the *sine qua non* of STORYNESS, this more Platonic definition focuses on the quintessential act of telling, dispersed though it is through "speaking agents".' (Ian Reid, 'Prospero meets Adam Smith: narrative exchange and control in *The Prelude*', a contribution to *Textual Practice*, summer 1987)

O those naughty, naughty neo-Aristotelian analysts! 'There was a boy, ye knew him well, ye lakes and islands of

Winander ...' what you didn't know was that you were non-speaking 'speaking agents' adding an exciting new dimension to *The Prelude*'s STORYNESS.

STRATEGY

noun. Any plan, however rudimentary, and be its aim never so flippant.

'Aramis introduces Nutriplexx, a survival STRATEGY for thinning hair.' (Advertisement in the *Evening Standard Magazine*, February 1988)

STREETWISE

adjective. Versed in the squalid expedients of petty urban crime. A word used freely by the sub-intelligentsia to suggest a canny toughness that is far from their true demeanour.

'A good cop has to be understanding, sympathetic, STREETWISE certainly, and humane, alert at all times.' (Peter Imbert, Chief Commissioner of Police, quoted in the *Evening Standard Magazine*, February 1988)

The London Bobby is not normally thought of as one of the sub-intelligentsia, but if Commissioner Imbert's advice about understanding, sympathy, and humanity bears fruit, there is yet hope.

STRIKE

verb. Deliberately to cultivate the superfluity of one's labour.

STRUCTURALISM

noun. An attempt to bring literature into line with the steel girder principles of modern architecture. (See POST-STRUCTURALISM)

STUBBLE BUZZ

noun. A sensation experienced by women whose paramours have neglected to shave, or have very short hair, or very, very short fingers.

'Drive Love Hamsters wild with ... shaved neck to give STUBBLE BUZZ ...' (*The Guide to Life, Part 8, Sex Technique*, in *Midweek*, 10.3.88)

No pleasure is without its attendant pain, and over-indulgence in STUBBLE BUZZ gives rise to a condition termed by the Americans, in their elegant way, 'razor burn'. (See BIKINI AREA.)

SUICIDE

noun. The grave offence of damaging government property.

SUPPLEMENTARY BENEFITS

noun. Small payments of doubtful benefit that supplement nothing at all.

SUPPORTIVE

adjective. Generously suppressing a strong inclination to deplore.

'Embarrassed at being labelled "Gorgeous George" the MP [George Galloway, Labour MP for Glasgow, Hillhead], tired and strained, slept late in his small Glasgow flat. Last night he met with [*sic*] his Party executive. "I found them to be warm and SUPPORTIVE" he said.' (Report in the *London Evening Standard*, 15.9.87, about Mr Galloway, who, the previous evening, had delighted the nation with an unscripted confession about his sexual affairs. It was not the sort of confession that would normally endear an MP to his party executive)

And:

'Politically Graham is extremely SUPPORTIVE; he gave up his holidays to act as my agent during the general election.' (Rosie Barnes, SDP MP for Greenwich, quoted in *The Times*, 2.3.88)

It seems that politicians stand in particular need of SUPPORTIVENESS.

But being SUPPORTIVE is not enough. Some higher level of aid and comfort is often required, and in these circumstances the elaboration 'supportative' has made its appearance. I recoil from the thought that this is merely an illiterate mistake, and I like to think that it indicates a better, higher, nay ENHANCED, degree of SUPPORTIVENESS.

SUITE

noun. A SUITE of rooms used to mean 'rooms joined together'. Nowadays it means ony one room, available for hire to EXECUTIVES.

Sometimes SUITES are called EXECUTIVE SUITES. Sometimes they are given resounding titles – the Westminster SUITE; the Lonsdale SUITE. Almost always they consist of one room. Quite a large room, to be sure, frequently equipped with audio-visual aids and other conference AMENITIES. More often than not there is an in-SUITE catering service available, and sometimes there is an entertainment FACILITY within the SUITE, from which a 'corporate hostess' can sally forth at intervals to refresh the parched EXECUTIVES.

But remember – do not expect more than one room in your SUITE. (See EN SUITE.)

SYMPOSIUM

noun. A supposedly dignified gathering which quickly degenerates into something more like its original meaning – to which the participants are delightfully oblivious – of a drinking bout.

SYNERGY

noun. Another technical term with a dazzling appeal to the sub-intelligentsia. It has several meanings, ranging from theology to pharmacology. The word implies the interaction of two or more elements with an effect greater than the sum of their separate effects. In anatomy it means 'the correlated action of a group of bodily organs', and in theology it means the co-operation of the human will and the Divine spirit to effect regeneration.

It is used by the pretentious to mean any co-operation of forces, however unimportant.

> ' ... permitting the SYNERGY of inter-departmental communication and other benefits associated with large buildings.' (J. Scott Lowry, chief ARCHITECT of the Canary Wharf development scheme in London's dockland, writing in *Property Now*, summer 1987)

Mr Lowry is trying to persuade his readers that their firms and companies would be far better off housed in one of his 'large buildings' at Canary Wharf. The picture he paints is of a company occupying offices so ERGONOMICALLY perfect that profitable interaction between the component parts of the company will be increased. But if he said so in plain words – 'Your company departments will co-operate better' – veteran sceptics would reply 'Like hell'. Much safer to go for SYNERGY.

T

TABLOID VIDEO

noun. A video-tape recording of base, crude and violent activities. What the American public has instead of gladiatorial contests. Christians and lions in your own sitting room. The natural offspring of CINEMA VERITÉ.

TABLOID derives from 'tablet', and was coined to describe newspapers printed on half-size sheets. Since such papers are usually taken up with sensationalism, TABLOID has come to refer in a general way to the vulgar press.

By enlarging the meaning of TABLOID to describe not only a college of the fourth estate, but also the murky topics in which it deals (as in TABLOID VIDEO), a bright hope for the future has been kindled.

The Americans, bored with fictional violence and corruption, have developed a taste for the real thing – not, as so often before, in the role of participants, but as spectators. Where video footage of actual violence is not available, some dark deed – a rape, or a mugging – is re-enacted (down to the last authenticated details) often by the original victims and assailants, who are then interviewed in exhaustive and salacious detail.

'Madison Avenue has found that one of its prime targets – women viewers aged under 49 – are particular fans of the new "TABLOID VIDEO".' (Report in *The Times*, 19.5.88)

The bright hope is, of course, that the

Americans will become so overstimulated by TABLOID VIDEOS that they will rush straight out and eradicate each other. But I also see a bright future for the word TABLOID itself As a general synonym for nasty, vulgar, brutish, and filthy it will greatly enhance the language:

'You 'orrible TABLOID little man!'

'When charged the accused responded with TABLOID ABUSE.'

'My God, war's a TABLOID business!'

And so on.

TACTICAL VOTING   *noun.* Voting for a representative you do not want to spoil the chances of one you want even less.

TAXATION   *noun.* A system of redistributing wealth to enable POLITICIANS to buy votes with your money.

TAX EFFICIENT   *adjective.* The quality of an investment portfolio which is too well bred to join the vulgar brawl of tax avoidance.

TECHNOLOGICAL   *adjective.* 'Technical' for those to whom technicalities are an impenetrable mystery.

TEENAGERS   *noun.* Those on whose behalf all the rights and privileges of full maturity are claimed. When shot or otherwise curbed by the forces of law, however, they automatically revert to the unqualified status of childhood.

TELEVISION   *noun.* The modern equivalent of the stocks. A cramped box in which petty malefactors are confined to suffer the derision of the mob.

TERMINATE

verb. To kill or murder. Properly speaking the usage should be 'to TERMINATE with extreme prejudice' – murder being only the most extreme mode of TERMINATION available to the world's spymasters. But the word has proved irresistible to the sort of mind that dwells on espionage, and in blockbusting BEST-SELLERS the world over the 'intelligence community' are hard at it, TERMINATING operatives all over the shop. In other words murdering their own agents as part of some larger plan. It is wholly characteristic of the twentieth century, that it should glamorise a figure which has been reviled and despised throughout history and in all civilisations – the spy.

TERRORISM

noun. Modern piracy. At first sight this might seem a wayward judgement, since pirates robbed and killed for gain, while TERRORISTS do so for allegedly political motives.

But the two callings have a crucial similarity – they have both been glamorised by the silly.

TEXTILE DEVELOPMENTS

noun. The abominable practice of allowing, and even encouraging, people to wear clothes, albeit of a vestigial kind. The term is used by NATURISTS whenever their right to nakedness is threatened.

'A gala day at South Hants which was threatened with closure but is now safe for 5 years more because PLANNERS said no to TEXTILE DEVELOPMENT.' (A caption in *Inland Free Sun*, a NATURIST guide, 1988)

'Hampstead Heath is costumes only now at the Highgate Pond & TEXTILES also rule supreme at Queensmere, Wimbledon. Liberated lesbians and press "revelations" put paid to the good old-fashioned innocence of Baden-Powell era.' (*Ibid.*)

THATCHERISM

noun. A set of political beliefs and activities associated with the British Prime Minister, Mrs Thatcher. The word is usually found in tandem with the pejorative 'uncaring'. It is Mrs Thatcher's greatest political asset that her face, voice and manner are entirely unable to express CARE or COMPASSION, thereby banishing her from the modern elect, and forcing her to consort with a frightful rabble called the electorate.

'The history of these early failures is easily forgotten in an era of THATCHERITE neo-LIBERALISM.' (Andy Green, *Marxism Today*, January 1988,

Mrs Thatcher is not often accused of LIBERALISM, neo or otherwise. The context suggests that this is Marxist code for 'letting the poor go to the wall.'

THEME PARK

noun. A piece of agriculturally and industrially valueless land, modified to divert the witless.

THE MOTORING EXPERIENCE

noun. The art of motoring in its widest context, embracing, in declining order of despair, the peculiar feeling on the steering, the smell of burning, the worsening rattle, the breakdown, the tow, the shaken head, the 'it's your bearings, innit', and last, but never least, The Bill.

THEOLOGY

noun. The study whose aim it is to justify the ways of men to God.

'The outstanding Anglican theological work in the last 30 years has in fact been liberal THEOLOGY ...' (Clifford Longley, *The Times* 22.2.88)

Or, in the case of liberal THEOLOGY. to criticise the ways of men to men.

THINGNESS   *noun.* The condition of being a thing.

' "Fashion and Surrealism" was a celebration of "THINGNESS": woman was a thing to be seen as if she were something else ...' (Deborah Drier, *Obsession, Art in America*, February 1988)

I have nothing to add. A celebration, in fact, of NOTHINGNESS.

THOUGHT-PROVOKING   *adjective.* Capable of making the thoughtless think that they have thought.

'Both THOUGHT-PROVOKING and original in approach, it is set to become the standard Shakespeare text for many years to come.' (Copy in The Folio Society's Special Publications brochure, advertising the Folio Shakespeare)

It would be an odd edition of Shakespeare's works that did not provoke thought, since the Swan of Avon was a dab hand in that line.

THROUGHPUT   *noun.* English for the American 'thru'put'. How INPUT becomes OUTPUT. Any continuous process in which something becomes something else.

To take an earthy example, the carnal act itself is not THROUGHPUT, since OUTPUT follows INPUT rapidly, in reverse direction, and with no intervening process. But the carnal act plus conception, plus pregnancy, plus delivery, represents THROUGHPUT in its most finished form – so finished that one can overlook the fact that the direction of travel is reversed, and 'throughness' is never entirely realised. But INPUT has become OUTPUT with a vengeance.

TIME SHARE

noun and *adjective*. 1. Playing Cox and Box with people whom mercifully you never have to meet.

2. A technique for selling the same property several times over to different buyers.

TRACK RECORD

noun. A modern curriculum vitae which, by its obvious reference to the world of sport, is intended to suggest tremendous energy and enthusiasm. There is also the implication that any TRACK RECORD must consist of wins, or at the worst second or third places. In the world of job applications the TRACK RECORD is usually an inspired work of fiction, dressing up a dismal catalogue of boredom and frustration as a triumphant career of interesting and impressive achievements.

'Candidates are sought with substantial experience of management in human services, resilience, imagination, FLAIR and a sense of humour. They should be able to demonstrate a good TRACK RECORD of CREATIVITY and achievement.' (Advertisement in the *Guardian*, 6.1.88., for a Deputy Director of Social Services in East Sussex)

What? Human resilience, human imagination, and human FLAIR as well?

TRAVELLER

noun. The words 'Gipsy' and 'Romany' are thought by the CARING to be pejorative, but TRAVELLER, with its associations of 'footloose', seems to me to be little better. Of course, with their extensive operations in the horse and scrap metal trades, it would be perfectly proper to call Gipsies 'travelling salesmen'.

TRUTH *noun.* ' "What is TRUTH?" said jesting Pilate', but it is no longer a jesting matter. TRUTH is a very desirable commodity, and everybody wants shares in it. The idea that TRUTH is what can be established by trial and error, or by an unbroken chain of reasoning, is hopelessly primitive and out of date. TRUTH is the prompting of your self-esteem, abetted by your imagination, and in unholy alliance with whatever system of BELIEF you adhere to.

But the word TRUTH is very useful to the connoisseur of modern nonsense – and some fairly ancient nonsense as well. Wherever TRUTH appears qualified by an adjective, there you are likely to find pretence, humbug, and thinly-disguised self or party interest.

So keep your eyes skinned for Revealed TRUTH, Catholic TRUTH, MARXIST TRUTH, Psychological TRUTH, Artistic TRUTH, and many other dawn raids on the helpless and diminishing stock of TRUTH.

U

UNIT

noun. A key word in constructing modern nonsense, almost *the* key word. It can be applied to anything, and I will not weary the reader with a list. It acquires its richest flavour of ambiguity when applied to organisations in which unity is very desirable, but not to be taken for granted. The military give us a good example by calling battalions of over 700 men UNITS.

UNIT COST

noun. Not what a UNIT costs you, but what it costs to manufacture. What such a desirable item costs you, the retail price, differs from the UNIT COST by a factor of many hundred per cent. And rightly so.

UNIT TRUST

noun. Don't.

UNLAWFUL WOUNDING

noun. Clubbing, stabbing or shooting your opponent without first joining the police force and being properly trained.

UP-MARKET

adjective. Nearer the stock market than the cattle market.

UPTURN

noun. The economic equivalent of a phantom pregnancy. A joyously awaited event which never arrives.

UPWARDLY MOBILE

adjective. Seeking to intensify your middle-class status.

URBAN PRIORITY AREAS

noun. Perhaps these are INNER CITIES, perhaps they are not. We can go no further than to say that they are tracts of townscape about which somebody wants to do something quickly.

' ... for having the foresight to set up a commission to investigate the plight of those who live in our URBAN PRIORITY AREAS.' (Letter to *The Times*, 8.12.87, signed, among others, by Graham Earney, 'Responsibility Officer' of the Diocesan Synod of Bath and Wells)

As a machine for generating farce, the Anglican Church has outstripped all other contenders. This letter was written in defence of Archbishop Runcie, who had been subjected to an anonymous attack, and it is his foresight which is celebrated.

Among other things, Dr Runcie's assailant said that the Anglican Church was neglecting its duty to teach the word of God and had, like sheep, gone astray into the lush but indigestible pastures of Social Concern, revelling in URBAN PRIORITY AREAS, and appointing Responsibility Officers left and right.

What *is* a Responsibility Officer?

This digression should not conceal that URBAN PRIORITY AREAS is a piece of nonsense. The compassionate are torn by two conflicting impulses. One is to emphasise the sufferings of the objects of their compassion, and the other is never to use a pejorative word in connection with them. They cannot, therefore, use the word 'slums', much as they would, from one point of view, like to. This is just as well, since the areas referred to, however run down, fall a long way short of the slum rookeries of Victorian England, or the cardboard and beercan huts of modern tropical cities.

So we've got URBAN PRIORITY AREAS instead. I can't help feeling they are just common or garden INNER CITIES.

USER-FRIENDLY

adjective. Having the desirable tendency not to maim or blind. A Labrador retriever represents the zenith of user-friendliness; a Spanish fighting bull its lowest point.

'Contents are genuine PET RUBBER: the first condom that's USER-FRIENDLY ... Plus: care and training booklet.' (Words printed on the packets of PET RUBBER, an American brand of contraceptive)

You mean all those Durex gossamer Nu-forms were user-hostile? As for a training booklet ...

'Standing properly Hat Hease, take the Rubber, Pet, one, in right hand, so ...'

V

VALORISATION

noun. When I came upon the extract quoted below, I immediately assumed that the author had invented this word. But it exists outside his tortured prose, and the *OED* defines it as 'fixing the price or value of a commodity, especially by a centrally-organised scheme.' Originating as it does in the world of money and business, it must surely be an illegal immigrant in this context.

'By the VALORIZATION of speech I mean that the discursive, circumstantially dense interchange of speaker facing hearer is made to stand – sometimes misleadingly – for a democratic equality and coprescence in actuality between speaker and hearer. Not only is the discursive relationship far from equal in actuality, but the text's attempt to dissemble by seeming to be open democratically to anyone who might read it is also an act of bad faith ... As Nietzsche had the perspicacity to see, texts are fundamentally facts of power, not of democratic exchange.' (Edward Said, *The World, the Text and the Critic*, Cambridge, 1983)

The confusion of democracy with equality places Mr Said firmly on the left, and – did we not know the left better – it would be curious to see him drawing inspiration from Friedrich 'the masses are muck' Nietszche. In his hands VALORI-SATION seems to mean that the expression of all argument, in speech or writing, is a wicked imposition on the hearer or reader. The alternative, of course, is silence, and one cannot help wishing that Mr Said would follow his ideas to their logical conclusion.

VALUE ADDED TAX   *noun.* A monstrous system of forced labour in which the self-employed are compelled to perform unpaid feats of accountancy on behalf of the Customs and Excise Department.

There is something gratuitously offensive about the use of the words VALUE and ADDED, almost as if you were being offered a bargain – cut-price cat food or suchlike. The VAT legislation, and the powers it confers on the VATmen, are the greatest injustice to have been inflicted on the British since the abolition of villeinage. In more honest times, compulsory, unpaid labour was called serfdom, but nowadays it is thought unkind to CIVIL SERVANTS to give their activities an honest name.

No hope can be looked for from a SOCIALIST government, since the burden of VAT falls on the self-employed and the small businessman. And no hope can be looked for from the CONSERVATIVES while they remain dominated by a clique which sees cost accountancy as the greatest – indeed the only – human virtue. As for the Liberals, can they even spell VAT?

VALUE DATE   *noun.* A notional moment – appointed unilaterally by a banker – before which he will not allow your contemptibly small sum of money to accrue any of the interest for which you have placed it in his care.

'Banking conducted after 3.30 p.m. will be VALUE DATED the following business day.' (A notice displayed in the bank Adams & Co., Pall Mall, London, November 1988)

It is quite typical of a banker to begrudge less than half a day's interest. It is equally typical that he is too ashamed of his base mentality to say outright 'I won't pay you any interest until tomorrow because it's inconveniently late in the afternoon.'

VANISHING SILHOUETTE

noun. What happens when your HIGH PROFILE sags.

VAPOUR WARE

noun. A computer program from which the program has been erased. It is therefore no longer even SOFTWARE, but has attained a state of disembodied purity.

VARIETAL

adjective. As an adjective derived from 'variety', VARIETAL might mean 'having variety'. But it is used by Californian wine growers as a solemn undertaking that their wines do *not* have variety. It means that the contents of the bottle come from only one, named, variety of grape.

This is a characteristic piece of American honesty, and one is grateful both for the wine and the honesty, if not for the unpronounceable word. But the French, who blend their grape varieties with frivolous abandon, and frequently resort to economies of truth in their labelling, continue to produce the world's best wines.

Is God trying to tell us something?

VERNACULAR

noun and *adjective.* Used of the disgraceful tendency of some POST-MODERN buildings to display bricks, timber, tiles and other unheard-of building materials.

VIABLE

adjective. Used as a loose synonym for 'possible' by those who suppose it to mean 'able to go' or 'able to make way'. Its real meaning – 'able to sustain life' – should be branded in letters of fire on the skulls of defence 'analysts' who talk of a 'viable nuclear deterrent'. It is interesting to reflect that a viable nuclear deterrent is almost certainly, in the same school of jargon, also a 'credible' nuclear deterrent. The least credible thing about it is that it could possibly be viable.

VIABLE is too useful a piece of nonsense to be confined to defence analysts. Feminists need it too:

'We make ourselves VIABLE by blocking out the everyday realization of how we have been emotionally deformed by our socialization ... '. (Meredith Tax writing in the anthology *Radical Feminism*, Quadrangle Books, New York, 1973)

Surely Meredith Tax is an assumed name? Anyway, what she means is 'we are able to cope by blocking out ...'

VOMIT

verb. Where previously to VOMIT was something disagreeable that you did yourself, it is now much more agreeable, having become something you can do to others.

'I VOMITED the dog and got back some liver ...' (A report in *The Times*, 15.2.88., about dog-doping at Crufts)

A very large predator – a tiger, or a leopard – that had feasted well but not wisely on somebody's dumb chum, would be able to 'vomit the dog', but not a veterinary surgeon, for such was the author of this remark. It is a pity that he should have fallen down so badly over VOMIT, because some lines further on he exhibits all the understated reserve we expect of dog lovers.

'I am particularly cross about this. It is an awful shame that this sort of thing is coming into dog fancying.'

W

WATERGATE

noun. A sally port, leading unexpectedly to a watershed.

WATER-RELATED

adjective. As the moribund docks of east London succumb to the developer, ARCHITECTS find themselves forced to adapt their simple grids to the canals of stagnant port water which intersect that derelict neighbourhood.

The necessity of making a wasteland appetising to the house buyer has fuelled the interesting evasion WATER-RELATED. Not every house can be said to enjoy a 'water frontage', a 'river frontage', or even a 'view of the river/water'. But most, so dank are the surroundings, can claim to be near water.

For some reason this is a great attraction to house buyers, who may be hoping to dispose of their unwanted young by drowning them (see RIGHT TO CHOOSE). Estate agents have therefore been quick to concoct the alluring phrase WATER-RELATED. It commits them to no more than the presence of water in the vicinity, but it suggests the picturesque on a Venetian scale.

The phrase is an advance on an earlier and cruder effort in the same vein, in which the vendor of a house, distant from the river bank by one block, described it as having 'an indirect river frontage'.

WELFARE STATE

noun. A form of social organisation in which the State fares well.

WE'RE TALKING ... HERE

no part of speech. 'WE'RE TALKING' can be transitive in the sense of 'WE'RE TALKING French', but to confuse it with 'we are discussing', or 'we are talking about' (and to tack on the unnecessary 'HERE') is wasteful, confusing and deliberately affected.

It usually appears in a phrase such as 'WE'RE TALKING big money HERE', or 'WE'RE not TALKING peanuts HERE'. In most cases 'WE'RE TALKING rubbish HERE' would be more accurate.

WHITE PAPER

noun. An example of modern ART at its most penetrating and subtle. One or more pieces of paper entirely covered in whitewash. The beholder is not expected to discover a meaning, but merely to marvel at the purity of the abstraction.

WILDWOOD

noun. Trees planted by the ecologically-minded.

'With others you will be *creating* a collectively owned WILDWOOD.' (Advertisement in *Marxism Today*, January 1988. [My italics])

WINE WAITER

noun. An immigrant worker who camouflages an absolute ignorance of wine with an equal command of English.

WORD PROCESSOR

noun. 1. A device for eliminating the class of employee who formerly had the impertinence to correct the English written by journalists.

2. A device for re-assembling English in forms acceptable to those who do not speak, write, or read it very easily.

WORKER *noun*. A fabulous being unceasingly invoked by POLITICIANS in the same way that superstitious people touch wood.

WORKFORCE *noun*. A body often prepared to use force to avoid working.

WORKSHOP *noun*. Used by the intelligentsia in an attempt to identify itself with the muscular proletariat. Theatre and dance workshops abound, but what goes on in them is so remote from what actually happens in a workshop that it is cruel to laugh.

WORK TO RULE *noun*. 1. The stage of an industrial dispute during which there is no rule and little work.
2. The intermediate stage between working haphazardly and not working at all indulged in by trade unions too timid to strike, but brazen enough not to mind the tacit admission that their rules are unworkable.

WORLD BEATING *adjective*. A meaningless piece of hyperbole roughly signifying 'best'. It is most prevalent among British sports commentators, whose predictions of WORLD BEATING potential are very rarely realised. Here is another proud WORLD BEATER from another field.

'an equity MARKET PLACE of WORLD BEATING potential is being established in London.' (Sir Nicholas Goodison, Chairman of the Stock Exchange, in the *Independent*, 21.4.87)

Two calamities befell the London Stock Exchange immediately before and after this confident statement. The first was the introduction, in 1986, of SEAQ – the Stock Exchange Automated Quoting System – amidst a great flurry of publicity, in the vein of 'we are the WORLD BEATERS'. It promptly broke down. The second was the collapse of equity prices in October 1987. The two phenomena are not entirely unconnected, and it is difficult to see where the WORLD BEATING comes in, though in fairness to Sir Nicholas it must be added that all the world's other stock markets suffered equally in the second calamity. Never let it be said, therefore, that the London Stock Exchange BEAT THE WORLD in ignorance, sloth, greed, and all the other amateurish bullshit that preceded the 1987 collapse.

WYSIWYG

no part of the speech. Pronounced 'Wizzy-wig'. The acronym of 'What You See Is What You Get'. Salesspeak for no frills, a straight deal, no hidden clauses. As modern speech regresses further into infantilism, we may expect more nursery-level acronyms.

Y

YUPPIE

noun. An extended acronym of 'Young UPWARDLY MOBILE Professional'. There is some dispute as to whether the U stands for UPWARDLY MOBILE or Urban. Either way YUPPIE is an indicator of class, and carries a strong undertone of disparagement.

In America where the term originated, to be young, UPWARDY MOBILE, and Professional is not necessarily a stigma. But enough residual idealism persists from the 60s to brand YUPPIES as too materialistic. In Britain YUPPIES are generally despised. To SOCIALISTS they are the heartless spawn of THATCHERISM. To Tories they are – well, not quite ... if you follow me. To Liberals and Social Democrats they are both.

Z

ZIONIST ENTITY   *noun.* The State of Israel, as figured in the mind of an Arab who finds it too painful to contemplate the reality of the Jewish nation, and therefore transmogrifies it into a less disconcerting abstraction – an entity – almost as if it were a plasmic cloud of Zionism that has momentarily settled on the Holy Land, soon to be wafted out to sea again.